CAREERS

VAULT GUIDE TO

VETERINARY AND ANIMAL CAREERS

VETERINARY AND ANIMAL CAREERS

The media's watching Vault! Here's a sampling of our coverage.

"For those hoping to climb the ladder of success, [Vault's] insights are priceless."
– ***Money*** **magazine**

"The best place on the web to prepare for a job search."
– ***Fortune***

"[Vault guides] make for excellent starting points for job hunters and should be purchased by academic libraries for their career sections [and] university career centers."
– ***Library Journal***

"The granddaddy of worker sites."
– ***U.S. News and World Report***

"A killer app."
– ***The New York Times***

One of Forbes' 33 "Favorite Sites."
– ***Forbes***

"To get the unvarnished scoop, check out Vault."
– ***Smart Money*** **Magazine**

"Vault has a wealth of information about major employers and job-searching strategies as well as comments from workers about their experiences at specific companies."
– ***The Washington Post***

"A key reference for those who want to know what it takes to get hired by a law firm and what to expect once they get there."
– ***New York Law Journal***

"Vault [provides] the skinny on working conditions at all kinds of companies from current and former employees."
– ***USA Today***

CAREERS

VAULT GUIDE TO

VETERINARY AND ANIMAL CAREERS

VETERINARY AND ANIMAL CAREERS

LIZ STEWART
and the staff of Vault

For information about permission to reproduce selections from this book, contact Vault.com, Inc., 75 Varick Street, New York, NY 10013, (212) 366-4212.

Library of Congress CIP Data is available.

ISBN 13 : 978-1-58131-548-6

ISBN 10 : 1-58131-548-1

Printed in the United States of America

ACKNOWLEDGMENTS

Liz Stewart's acknowledgments: I would like to thank Vault for adding the animal career industry to its list of guides and, in particular, my editor, Matthew Thornton for the help and guidance he has given to me as a novice writer. I thank my family for supporting my love for animals, including my job in the veterinary field and the strange hours I keep there! I also thank the Oradell Animal Hospital for its continued commitment to the veterinary community. I feel fortunate to be part of this team of caring professionals with whom I continue to grow and learn.

Vault's acknowledgments: We are extremely grateful to Vault's entire staff for all their help in the editorial, production and marketing processes. Vault also would like to acknowledge the support of our investors, clients, employees, family and friends. Thank you!

Table of Contents

Chapter 4: Major Employers 37

GETTING HIRED 47

Chapter 5: Education 49

Chapter 6: Getting Your Foot in the Door 65

Chapter 7: Resumes and Cover Letters 73

Introduction

What is a Career with Animals?

Careers with animals encompass a large range of options, from working in kennels and vet offices to farming and ranching. Becoming a veterinarian is one of many avenues for the scientifically inclined. If you're science-oriented, you might also work with animals in research to find cures for diseases and to develop new medicines for the animals themselves, or for humans.

Not just science

But that's not all. If you're interested in business or management, jobs from farming to grooming to pet daycare operations require those skills. (Particularly if you open your own business and have people working under you, accurate financial records, reporting of earnings and record-keeping in general are essential. In some industries, you will be required to go through inspections of your facilities and business operations.)

Many animal-related careers presume a certain degree of environmental and social awareness. If you have a strong sense of global responsibility, you may be motivated to take on challenges facing animals in local communities or throughout the world through an organization like the ASPCA, a group that is dedicated to promoting the welfare of animals through education and adoptions of animals.

All for the love of animals

Whatever the career, people who work with animals are usually drawn to the field through a natural sense of bonding with animals that developed at an early age. For that reason, careers with animals can offer a sense of fulfillment that other jobs often don't.

Is this the Right Field for You?

Basic requirements

It's critical to be honest about your abilities, emotionally, physically, educationally and financially. When working with animals, you are dealing with living beings, and this can happen in different capacities. Working in an animal hospital setting involves healing patients, whereas a laboratory may use animals for the sole purpose of gaining information. These positions are mentally and physically challenging. Veterinarians must be able to communicate with clients in a clear, compassionate way while assessing diagnostic tests to come up with a medical plan. Cases don't always go as planned, and doctors often have to reassess patient status throughout the course of a day. They then need to communicate these updates to the client.

It may be hard for some people to emotionally watch or do tasks involved with each job; for example, two common procedures in both veterinary medicine and scientific fields involving animals are surgery and humane euthanasia. These procedures are not for the queasy or highly emotional. On a ranch or farm, there may be hard decisions to make about animal health or the sale of animals for food. Even if you're pet sitting, you may come upon an emergency situation that requires quick, educated, level-headed decision-making. You must have the ability to read basic animal body language, and learn how to approach and handle animals accordingly. You must also have a strong physical constitution to deal with the daily physical demands of most of these jobs. Some require heavy or repetitive lifting, bending, standing on your feet all day with no or little time for breaks, or you may need to endure harsh environmental conditions outdoors.

People whisperer

Animal careers also involve working with other people, so good communication skills are needed. Even if you are not dealing directly with clients, such as in a laboratory or zoo setting, you will still need to communicate the needs of the animals and convey ideas or concerns you may have to those you work with. In a zoo, even if you do exclusively kennel work, you'll need to effectively convey any change in a patient's status to the technician or veterinarian.

Getting there

There are almost limitless possibilities when choosing a career involving animals. Picking the right one may happen right away, or may take years of trying out various jobs to find the right fit. Many positions require years of schooling, training and experience. The ultimate fulfillment in these jobs often comes from the contact with the animals. Despite all the ups and downs, the sight of a puppy's tail wagging, the experience of a bright sunny day on the farm, a difficult surgery that saved a life or the discovery of the cure for a disease and knowing you made a difference is what drives people to work with animals.

CAREERS

THE SCOOP

VETERINARY AND ANIMAL CAREERS

The Evolving Role of Animals in Society

CHAPTER 1

A Brief History

The greatness of a nation and its moral progress can be judged by the way its animals are treated

—Mahatma Gandhi

Animals and religion

Animals have been thought of by humans in many different ways over time. In the ancient Rome of Shakespeare's *Julius Caesar,* the augurers, similar to today's fortunetellers, would read the entrails of animals to make predictions and give advice to people about their future. Going back to ancient civilizations, the religious belief that ancestors returned in animal form, and must be worshipped in that form, is prevalent. Certain religions thought of animals as powerful gods that should be revered. If people did not behave a certain way in their living life, they would be tormented by these animal spirits who would sometimes haunt these wrongdoers into the next life. If people lived as they should, the animal spirits would reward them and their tribe with a bountiful existence.

These were times when humans saw themselves as part of the cycle of nature, not separate from it. Because people lived in such constant contact with nature and the animals they encountered, there was an awe and respect of the world and the animals that inhabited it. Some religions today, like the Hindu Jain sect, still have a respect for animals; followers do not practice any act that would harm an animal. These strict vegetarians wear scarves over their faces so that no insects fly into their mouths to be accidentally swallowed and killed. In India, cows are worshipped and are allowed to roam freely without harm from people. Certain Buddhists gently sweep the ground in front of them as they walk to ensure that before they take a step there is not a living being that would be crushed under their feet.

Myth and Reality

Folklore has always featured animals and their powers as archetypes; human traits and qualities are given to animals to prove a lesson. One of the oldest stories involving animals is that of Noah's Ark, in which God tells Noah to build a boat and bring two of each animal to start a new world after the flood. It is a dove who brings the message that the flood has ended, an animal that still represents peace in today's world. This and other stories, which are still told today in one form or another, underscore how humans continue to have a need to relate to creatures in nature.

This has played out in numerous ways throughout recent history. Animals have been used as gruesome entertainment, such as in cock fights or bull fighting. Circuses have employed wild animals, keeping them in small enclosures and encouraging them to perform unnatural tricks for the audience. Animals appear regularly in advertising, television and movies, and have even been used for communication purposes, with hawks or homing pigeons being sent off for delivery with written messages tied to their feet.

Animals as tools

As civilizations grew and cultures began to clash, animals were used in war as sources of transportation, carrying troops onto the battlefield, moving weapons and even as decoys, such as the infamous Trojan horse, which was built in the guise of a present for the enemy. Mascots, in the form of animals, were often used to show the power of a particular troop, and they were often brought along when marching to a battlefield to keep the troops' spirits up, to alert them when danger was approaching and to keep them company. Animals were sometimes traded as commodities between both warring and peaceful cultures.

Indigenous peoples used animals to survive, seeing themselves as part of the natural cycle of life and using their resources accordingly. Animals were useful for protection, food, clothing or tools and as cultures developed, so did animals' roles. The Native Plains Indians of North America began to use horses for transportation and when hunting. Every piece of the animals they hunted and caught was used for food, clothes, shelter and tools; nothing went to waste. Various animals were worshipped in rituals, in which the Indians would ask for protection, shelter and food from the animal spirits. Watching the behavior of animals, these people believed themselves able to tell if a change was coming, and acted accordingly.

Animals and agriculture

Agriculture is one industry that has steadily relied on the use of animals in the same basic way, and people who owned animals had to know how to care for them. Nomadic tribes would sometimes move herds of animals as they relocate to new living space, maintaining a kind of roaming farm. Some cultures still use animals to measure a family's wealth relative to their community. Their animals may be traded for other goods or used to pay things such as dowries for a son or daughter's wedding.

Small family farms have always depended on animals to run the operation. Before motorized equipment, animals pulled plows, for instance. Dogs would protect the property while cats would control the vermin. Cows and sheep grazed the pastures, keeping them from becoming overgrown while at the same time fertilizing the soil. Various farm animals provided milk, meat and eggs to use and sell. In return, the farm animals were protected from predators and given a steady diet. The relationship was more or less compatible.

More recently, farming has become increasingly corporatized as the public's demand for farm products increased. Mechanized farming equipment has done away with the labor-intense farm practices of the 20th century and, as a result, there are fewer small, family-owned rural farms and ranches and more large corporate factory farms. In effect, more people moved away from their farming families to join the urban population and make more money to live. This has led to some problems. In factory farming, animals are often forced to live in small, filthy cages. They may be given hormones to make them grow faster and bigger, and antibiotics to control the infections developed from lowered immune systems from stress or from practices such as being debeaked or having their tails cut short. Today, family farmers are still struggling against complete corporate takeover, and seem to have made some headway, reclaiming their right to treat farm animals and the land with more respect. There has also been a push from consumers for products from animals that are treated more humanely. Consumers are also more aware of the increased health threat to the food supply and inhumane, unethical treatment of animals that can occur as a result of factory farming.

Taking Care of Our Animals

The first vets

Middle Eastern cultures as far back as 4000 B.C. that kept herds of sheep or horses were thought to understand animal physiology and disease processes. The Egyptians kept records showing they used medicine on their dogs and horses alongside the practice of human medicine, whereas ancient Indian art shows humans caring for horses and elephants. The first veterinary school, known as the Royal Veterinary School, was created in Lyon, France in 1761. Studies provided students anatomical and disease information about horses, cattle and sheep. In America, the first established accredited veterinary school was the School of Veterinary Medicine at the University of Pennsylvania in 1883.

Animal welfare

As the world became industrialized, resources were thought of differently and, with it, the role of animals changed. People no longer relied as much on the natural world around them, and they could obtain resources fairly easily at the local market. People became more removed from the source of their food and supplies, and as time went on, they began to forget how it got there. At the same time, an increasing number of people were no longer tied down to tending a farm, or even having to contribute to society in the same way. In an industrial society, people now had a choice about how to treat their animals. Animal welfare organizations sprung up in response, with the first documented in 1822, when British Parliament passed a bill that gave protection from cruelty to cattle, horses and sheep. This bill paved the way for the SPCA (Society for the Prevention of Cruelty to Animals), formed in 1824, to focus on the way humans treated the animals they lived and interacted with.

New York City developed its first animal cruelty society, the ASPCA, in the late 1800s, to lobby the government-run shelters on behalf of humane treatments for animals. This organization eventually took over the government-run program and today continues to promote anticruelty within the animal world, in the private and public sector.

Breeding

Breeding was popularized in the Victorian era some 150 years ago, though horse breeding, in particular, has a longer history. The Middle Eastern Bedouins kept written pedigrees of Arabian horses from 1330 A.D., and an oral record of this breeding extends further back. Horses were bred in Mongolia for both war and racing, and the thoroughbred horse was developed in Britain in 1660; prior to that horseracing had been banned.

Industry Trends

CHAPTER 2

As we become wealthier, we become more removed from the natural world. Industrialization has created a mechanical world separate from the natural world where it appears we no longer depend on the land or animals for our survival. But we are not separate from nature, as the increased political emphasis on climate change shows. TV programs such as *Nature* have shifted away from a biological point of view to an ecological one. Numerous documentaries and articles have also explored how climate change is affecting animal populations. It's unclear whether increased awareness of our natural resources plays a role in this, but according to the U.S. Department of Labor, jobs involving animals have grown in demand of late. This is particularly true in the area of small animal care, though the veterinary field is also projected to grow.

Dearly Beloved Pets

Pet ownership is also burgeoning, and with a strong economy, humans have the luxury of keeping animals as companion pets, often ranking them as important members of the family. In some cases, they are thought to be a substitute for children or are considered to be a person's only family; recently, it was revealed that deceased hotel magnate Leona Helmsley willed a sizable fortune to her dog.

Low maintenance pets

These days, cat ownership is growing in larger numbers, as many people are finding it hard to commit to the routine of owning a dog. Rabbits and ferrets are also popular smaller pets that possess some traits of dogs and cats. According to the AVMA 2001 *U.S. Pet Ownership and Demographic Sourcebook*, since 2004, small animal and reptile ownership has grown by over two million in population. Small living spaces and rules that keep dogs and cats out of rented places may have an impact on decision making, as more people are turning to snakes, lizards and birds as pets.

The cost of pet ownership

According to the American Pet Product Manufacturing Association, pet-related spending has doubled over the past 10 years, and this statistic is reflected both in flourishing veterinary practices as well as those, unfortunately, of animal shelters. The veterinary field has been experiencing a growth spurt recently, as more people are willing to pay a high price for their pet's health care. An average health checkup can cost hundreds of dollars (this includes the exam, preemptive screening blood work and vaccines) to tens of thousands for referral and emergency cases for pets that need veterinary specialists, various diagnostic testing, surgery and 24 hour hospitalization in a critical care unit. One remedy for these rising costs has been pet health insurance, developed over the past 10 years, and offered through the ASPCA or other independent companies. Popular with pet owners, insurance plans may cover vaccines, emergencies and other basic treatment depending on the policy. But many pet owners are still willing to pay for their pet's heath needs beyond what pet insurance offers, which keeps the vet industry growing. With the cardiac, respiratory, orthopedic and other problems that some of the specialty breeds present, the veterinary industry has started looking towards human medicine to develop the same quality of care for their animal counterparts.

With the massive growth in pet ownership comes a large number of people not being able to handle the responsibility. In 1997, 4.3 million animals were handled by 1,000 shelters that responded to a survey done by the National Council on Pet Population and Study. These unwanted pets are brought to animal shelters because of people's misconception of what the experience would be like. Shelters and rescue groups have become important parts of our society (there are well over five thousand shelters nationally that each hold at least 100 animals) where many unwanted pets are given a second chance.

Training the perfect pet

For those who do stick with their new pet, training often becomes necessary. According to pet manufacturing groups, pet ownership in the U.S. is up from 51 million homes to 69 million homes since 1988 with more homes taking in multiple pets in greater numbers. And a surprising number of these new owners have never previously had close interactions with pets and may not have good intuition as to how to raise a well-mannered dog. These owners look to trainers to help them mold their new puppies, or to help reverse bad traits that have already developed. All dogs do not have the same personalities, and as breeds of dogs are changing, so are their temperaments. With the breeding of 150 different types of dogs recognized and listed by the AKC—with up to 400 breeds that are not officially recognized—comes the need for trainers to identify the best way to control these different personalities. With this increased unpredictability, many new pet owners don't accurately estimate the amount of time they will need to spend with their dog to train it properly.

Breeding

Specialty breeding

Animal breeding has become extremely specialized in some areas of the world and among certain status groups. Today, a number of breeds, from Shar-Peis to bulldogs, are bred for a certain look. These kinds of smaller breeds are increasingly popular, perhaps because of an increase in apartment dwellers, but in certain cases small breeds have cache. Chihuahuas, for example, have become a status symbol of celebrities, who carry them in their expensive purses, which encourages fans to mimic the same trend. But creating a smaller version of a dog can be associated with heart problems and other metabolic diseases. The problem with this specializing is that there tends to be a trade off for health and the newly engineered breed may be genetically predisposed to more medical problems than a mixed breed would. Shar-peis, now bred with more wrinkles, have experienced excessive skin problems and eye problems, whereas bulldogs have increased respiratory ailments because of breeding that encourages pushed-in faces. The King Charles Cavalier has been bred to have a smaller snout and dome head, which has caused some degree of heart disease in those dogs.

Puppy mills

In contrast, backyard breeding is when two animals are allowed to breed indiscriminately, ignoring any genetics, aesthetics or physical health. The term "backyard breeder" is used to refer to a smaller-scale operation; when done on a larger scale, the business is called a "puppy mill." At one time, it was common for a family farmer or a neighbor to breed their dog and the neighbors would all go to them for puppies. Today we continue to use selective breeding, adding to the over 400 dog breeds already recognized around the world. There are more specialized breeds or dogs with new breeds (not necessarily registered with a breed club) constantly being developed, like labradoodles, pom-a-poos and puggles, for specific traits such as allergen-free fur or being pocket-sized.

Some breeders have responded by breeding and marketing certain types of dogs to pet stores. These breeders are usually associated with the aforementioned "puppy mills," which are completely consumer-driven. Pet stores located in malls or on highway shopping strips sell these "puppy mill" puppies and cater to consumers who impulsively buy there, often spending more than they would have if they bought directly from a registered breeder. Often, these "puppy mill" puppies are poorly bred, and although they may cost more than a puppy from a reputable breeder, they come with a myriad of medical problems. Illnesses resulting from cramped living spaces in puppy mills with other sick animals (similar to the well-documented problems of factory farms) include respiratory problems and infectious gastrointestinal diseases like Parvovirus. In some cases, a puppy must then be treated at the vet for several days, often costing the new owner hundreds to thousands of dollars.

The Humane Society of the United States, AKC, ASPCA and many other grassroots groups connected to the numerous shelters across the country advocate against puppy mills. These groups work to educate the public and encourage people to responsibly research buying a puppy from a responsible breeder, but until regulation of puppy stores is tightened, the sales will continue.

The Evolution of Zoos

Zoos used to be places to view exotic animals that were transported from far away places and were then caged in a small, cramped, unnatural setting. As the world's natural places become scarcer, the role of the zoo has changed. The environments where the zoo animals are housed have become better representations of animals' natural habitats, and working in zoos increasingly require staff to know more about an animal's natural habitat, not just their behavior.

Zoos for the environment

Zoos are also actively involved in environmental and preservation initiatives. The San Diego Zoo, one of the leading American zoos, cooperates in breeding programs to preserve certain declining species, such as the giant pandas, tigers, black-footed ferrets and Asian elephants. Workers in zoos involved in these kinds of programs may be employed in various transportation, introduction, paperwork and funding capacities for these programs. In National Parks like Yosemite, wildlife management workers monitor the land to ensure that people are not abusing the grounds, and wildlife rehabilitators work with injured native mammals and birds too young to care for themselves. These animals are either released if they are able to survive in their natural habitat, or are kept protected in a wild setting at a nature center or zoo for the remainder of their lives.

Zoo education

Zoos are also increasingly emphasizing education, with online and in-house educational resources and children's education programs and camps available. Many, like the National Zoo Park in Washington, DC, cooperate with local museums to continue teaching the public about these animals. Although jobs within zoos can be scarce and the competition fierce, there are volunteer jobs available within these educational areas.

Ecotourism and Animal Education

Animal education for the public is now often achieved through professionally produced documentaries. Long gone are the antiquated shots from Mutual of Omaha's Wild Kingdom series with Marlon Perkins. Today, we are able to view scenes up close, underground, high in tree tops or in time-lapse. In fact, scientists now use GPS devices to help track and understand animal populations. The amount of knowledge about animals gained over the years by naturalists has helped us in understanding how all systems depend on each other to survive.

Ecotourism is increasingly popular as people want to see these exotic places. Though travel has become easier, many of these destinations, from the Galapagos in South America to penguin-inhabited polar icecaps, enforce a limited amount of tourists each day to maintain the balance of the land. Ecotourism has also created a new job market, and whereas most of these jobs would fall into the category of park ranger, overseas there are opportunities to either work or find internships or volunteer jobs. According to the International Tourism Club, there are at least 200 job vacancies available at any given time through their web site.

Science and Research

Historically, animals have been used in research to mimic the effect of an experiment within a living system, thus saving humans from having to sacrifice themselves for experiments. Laboratory research is now regulated by strict guidelines and is supervised by boards such as the National Association for Biomedical Research with regard to how animals are treated. In cases where other methods can be used, animals are largely left out of the experiments. From an educational standpoint, many schools that previously used animals to teach students in their laboratories now look to computer models to teach the same points, sparing the lives of many research animals like beagles and monkeys. Jobs within the research field now include those dealing with regulation of how animals are treated, and the conducting of regular inspections. Laboratory staff may require more training and education than in the past because of these strict regulations.

The scientific community continues to look at animals as indicators as to how to look at human medical problems differently. One question that increasingly arises is that of aging. For instance, turtle organs do not age even as they approach 200 years old. A number of scientific and biological research jobs, typically at universities, involve studying these animals and their biological curiosities to help create solutions to aging in humans.

Farming and Genetics

Over the past century, corporations have introduced elements of a factory environment to the farming industry to raise farm animals more cheaply. As a result, small farmers have suffered financially, forcing them to sell their land and equipment or take on part time jobs to support their farms. But increased environmental awareness has translated to an increased consumer concern over where their food comes from. Studies and reports have indicated that factory farm animal genetics have been tampered with to the point where using these animals for food may be unsafe. For example, cows in factory farms are typically house in dirty, cramped conditions, causing them stress. To keep them from becoming sick, they are fed antibiotics. To make these cows produce more milk or muscle, they are also given growth hormone. These antibiotics and steroids end up in the final product, which is then eaten or drunk by consumers. In response, informed consumers are looking for organic and more environmentally friendly alternatives from farmers. Small farmers are beginning to see that they need to market themselves differently to compete with corporate farming industries. Therefore, larger farm jobs are on the decline, whereas smaller specialty farms are on the rise. Farmers' markets have become increasingly popular across the country for locally grown fruits and vegetables as well as dairy and other products, and small farms have started marketing themselves within their communities, holding family days for visits and educational tours of their farms.

Otherwise, the number of jobs in farming is expected to decrease, according to the U.S. Department of Labor, because of an increasing reliance on mechanized equipment.

Becoming a Vet: Specialization

If there's a trend in terms of vet careers themselves, it's further specialization. Veterinary graduates often do intern and residency programs gaining boarding in a specialty. From there, they may open their own specialty practice, work per diem for other local clinics or work for larger hospitals as part of a specialty staff.

Pet owner therapist

Veterinary practices have also expanded their services. Grief support help lines and pet loss psychological services for people who have a hard time coping after losing a pet are now being offered through hotline telephone support or community outreach programs with a bereavement councilor co-ordinating the sessions via veterinary offices.

Even a new specialty of pet lawyers is emerging to help people who have legal issues involving their pets like apartment housing in rent stabilized areas, bite cases, malpractice suits or ownership issues.

Jobs in the Animal Field

CHAPTER 3

Although the relationship between humans and animals has evolved throughout history, animals are still an important part of the human world, even if we are not a necessary part of theirs. So as long as there are animals in our world, we need to care for them. Accordingly, jobs in the animal fields are constantly changing and continue to be on the rise. The following chapter describes many types of jobs available to someone who wants to work with animals and will lay out further information about the education and training needed for each particular career.

Finding the right fit

Because there are many types of jobs within the animal career category, you should research the particular animal field you are interested in to see if it fits your lifestyle, monetary needs, and if it is compatible with what you are able to physically and mentally do. Obviously, there are some fields of interest, like biomedical research, that do not offer volunteer or entry level positions to test it out. In these cases, it is worth the time to look into setting up an observation so that you can see for yourself what is involved. You can also seek out volunteer or entry level jobs similar to the field you are looking into, even if it is not exactly the same job you eventually want to be in. Many veterinary students will work in a veterinary clinic as a veterinary assistant or technician, gaining experience and skills, until they graduate from veterinary school. Although the jobs are not the same, they are able to gain an understanding of what it is like to work in that type of environment.

As there are differences within the animal career industry, it is best to leave your options open until you find a path that you know you want to take. You may have an animal science degree and have a job on a horse breeding farm, but are waiting for an opening as a caretaker in a zoo. If you have dog grooming experience, you may handle dogs for a breeder who shows her dogs, while still doing grooming on the side. There are country veterinarians who still make house calls and care for both domestic pets and farm animals as opposed to veterinarians who prefer to work in a laboratory setting reading pathology slides.

Basic preparation

Working with animals is almost always physically and emotionally demanding. You must be compassionate, and also have a strong work ethic and problem solving skills. Starting out, you will need to learn how to read an animal's subtle body language to predict its behavior and will need training on how to handle the particular animals you will be dealing with. Basic math skills are required for most jobs in animal fields as is some basic biology and anatomy. Familiarity with medical terminology can also be useful.

Some people have always known that they want to work with animals and begin in that direction at an early age by joining local 4-H clubs or by raising their own pets. For most careers involving animals, it helps to have taken courses in the sciences and maths. Many high schools now have work study programs where students spend part of their day in a real job situation. Animal hospitals are good hosts for this kind of program. Other high schools have actual vocational schools with dog grooming and handling classes, in which students learn a hands-on career, learning how to groom or care for animals in conjunction with a local veterinarian or grooming business.

Education

In college, a course of study in the animal or biological sciences, which are available in most schools, is a good start and can lead to degrees in pre-veterinary medicine, research or farm management. For more specific career paths, such as in zoology or biological sciences, you'll need an advanced degree. Either way, it's definitely beneficial to find a job in the animal field before or while attending college classes not only to give you hands-on experience, but to confirm that you're going in the right direction. Some people graduate college with a degree in some type of animal field only to discover later it is not the lifestyle or job they pictured.

If you have not started along the animal career path early and you've decided to change careers and need further education to start in the animal field, look into local college programs or online degrees. This way you can keep working at a current job as you work towards your degree in the chosen animal field. But do some research first to make sure any degrees you obtain will be viable for the job you are ultimately looking for. For example, to become a veterinary technician, any program you graduate from must be accredited by the AVMA for you to be able to sit for the National Veterinary Technician Exam to become certified. If you then gain an entry-level position as an assistant in an animal hospital, you will be getting the hands-on experience needed that would not be offered by long distance learning.

Now we will discuss more specific education needed for certain animal careers to help you on your way.

Veterinarian

A veterinarian examines, diagnoses and treats patient medical conditions. According to the veterinary oath, veterinarians are sworn "to protect animal health and relieve animal suffering." Along with possessing compassion for animals, individuals must have a scientific, problem-solving mind as well as the ability to physically accomplish medical procedures while communicating to their clients. A large part of small animal veterinary practice includes dealing with clients, and communication skills are an important, yet often a neglected, part of a veterinarian's training.

For veterinarians, there is a limitless range of possibilities available as far as types of work environments, types of hours and types of work available. Of course, at the beginning of a career, more time is spent gaining experience, which usually requires working longer hours with less pay. As a veterinarian becomes more experienced and gains more certifications, he or she has more of a choice as to what type of position he or she would like. Just as in human medicine, veterinary general practitioners see basic appointments, checking the overall health of the patient, giving vaccines, doing basic screening tests, consulting about feeding requirements and answering client questions.

According to the U.S. Department of Labor, the outlook for jobs in the veterinary field is good. The combination of the limited number of vet programs (there are only 28 nationally, thus limiting the number of veterinarians graduating from school) and the increased consumer need for veterinarians guarantee continued job availability.

Kinds of practices

Jobs can vary depending on type of practice. Some small clinics may have two to three general practitioners, whereas large university teaching hospitals include both specialists and student training. In a smaller practice, a general veterinary practitioner calls upon basic knowledge of all specialties to begin to diagnose their patients. He must also be aware of differences within animal species, as treatment for a cat may not be the right treatment for a ferret. Often, when a general practitioner feels like a sick animal needs more diagnostic work or intense nursing care, he will refer the patient to a larger hospital that employs specialists.

A referral practice may be privately owned or may be part of a public institution such as a university hospital. These larger teaching hospitals usually run 24 hours a day, 7 days a week, and offer a full range of staff and caseloads. Larger hospitals retain experienced staff specialists and offer internship, externship and other training programs for vets. Some doctors work alone, making house calls, whereas others are solely available for consultations to other hospitals. Many of these veterinarians choose to open their own clinics and have to juggle between practicing medicine and running a business, although running a hospital efficiently while seeing clients, evaluating patients and doing medical procedures can be challenging. Hiring an office manager allows the doctor to continue his or her job without putting in long hours to run the practice.

Specialties

Certain specialties, such as emergency and critical care or surgery, inherently require a flexible schedule. After-hour emergency cases and surgeries are always needed any time of day. In a shelter or zoo, veterinarians may be required to check in on the weekends. Because so many practices are trying to compete with larger hospitals, they may hire veterinarians per diem to lighten their case load or to cover off-hour, holiday or vacation schedules. Specialty veterinarians who travel to clinics can often set their own work time. They may be able to do their consults over the phone or on-line, as radiologists do. Behaviorists usually have their own business, but may have associations with certain hospitals that refer clients to them. Research and laboratory veterinarians usually have more traditional schedules during the work week, but may spend time at night attending meetings which help to regulate their industry. Farm and country doctors need variable schedules and usually have mixed practices, seeing both farm and companion animals. They are usually required to be on call all the time.

Veterinarians who work in zoos or wildlife facilities have already gained experience in small animal medicine. The competition for these jobs is stiff, because of the limited number of positions and large pool of interested applicants. Completing an internship, although maybe not directly related to zoo medicine, may help to secure a job in this area. Externships are also available in certain zoos or facilities, but are just as competitive because of the limited spaces available and large pool of applicants. Working in a zoo or wildlife facility requires specific knowledge about the animals to be handled and treated. Veterinarians in these fields often benefit from research grants designated for the study of animals in their natural habitat. One thing to keep in mind is that veterinarians who work in these areas may be required to travel or relocate frequently.

Growing areas of interest in the veterinary field include physical therapy, behavior, feline medicine, dentistry, dermatology, exotics, zoo medicine (including aquariums) and wildlife rehabilitation. Government jobs are also on the rise, resulting from the growing public concern over human and animal welfare, zoonotic diseases and food safety.

Veterinarians at the top of their field are typically sought after for their experience, and may become frequent lecturers or journal writers contributing case studies to the field. Both new and established veterinarians may choose to focus more of their training in the business and management side of running a veterinary practice. Most states, by law, only allow a credentialed veterinarian to own veterinary practices, although some states only require a veterinarian to be on site while someone else may own the practice.

Support staff

Doctors usually have a support staff of receptionists, veterinary technicians and kennel help, which allows them to provide overall care to a patient. Support staff positions are filled by a mix of people who either work their way up in the field, are currently enrolled in a veterinary technology degree program, or others who are making change-of-life careers.

Breeding

Animals usually thought of as being bred are dogs, horses, cats and rabbits, although any animal can be bred, including those bred for specific traits used by research facilities.

Dogs (and cats)

If you want to breed as a part time or full time endeavor, your first order of business should be to research the subject thoroughly and talk to breeders in your area. For dog breeding, a good place to start is the American Kennel Club (AKC), which is the largest dog breed club, recognizing over 150 breeds. The Cat Fanciers' Association, Inc. recognizes 39 pedigrees of cats. There are also several dog and cat clubs specific to certain breeds, such as the Jack Russell Terrier Association of America (JRTCA) and researching these groups is a good idea too. You should be prepared to attend dog and cat shows in your area; these shows are usually held seasonally during the spring, summer and fall, and they're a good place to talk to breeders about getting started. You will eventually need to develop a good working relationship with other trusted people like handlers, other club members, and office staff of the particular club within the breeding world. These people are valuable sources of information and can help diversify your breeding stock with genes from their animals. They will also be handy in helping to find homes when it comes to selling the animals.

Getting started

If you are lucky enough to find a breeder locally to work with, the experience will be a valuable one. Many breeders have passed on their knowledge within their family and have years of experience that you can only acquire hands-on. Another way to get started is to find a reputable breeder and purchase a breeding dog from them, allowing you to develop a working relationship with them.

Once you are decided on what kind of animal you will be breeding, you will need to start with a breeding pair. Some breeders will sell a female under contract, which gives that breeder pick of the first litter born. This can be a good way to start a breeding program, as the breeder you work with should want to be involved in certain aspects of the breeding, birth and sale of the young. The breeder can help you arrange for a stud dog, give advice as needed throughout the pregnancy and help draw up pedigrees and sale contracts. The breeder should also have connections in facilitating the sale of the young. You will need to make the mother and young the focus of your time, and you'll need to spend a lot of time and money setting up a proper environment with supplies, food and trips to the veterinarian. Any breeder you work with should be willing to teach and share information with you. People who are in this field and are well-established realize the benefit to promoting good breeding within the industry.

How do you know a breeder's for real?

Do note that there is currently no licensing regulation of breeders within the United States, technically making anyone out there with a pregnant animal a breeder. Specific breed clubs will often recommend carefully screened breeders to the public. Many good breeders do not get into this field for the money, although over time as they earn a reputation, they may do well financially. Very often people who have money and are looking for a hobby get into this type of selective breeding.

Showing

Breeders who begin showing their animals in competitions may employ dog handlers, another offshoot of this career. Handlers tend to be used by top breeders to show their champions at a high level of competition. There is also training, which typically involves veterinarian behaviorists who observe a client with their pets (or within a facility such as a zoo) and are able to recommend a course of action. (The analogy for humans would be psychologist.) If needed, these trainers are also able to prescribe medications to help facilitate the treatment.

The AKC offers information on breeding and how to contact specific breed clubs to reseach their member breeders. Much research is needed in order to start up properly in this field; reading up on the subject, making phone calls to clubs and breeders for information and attending club events are the best ways to get started.

Other kinds of breeding careers

Breeding careers, a natural for animal science majors, also include farming for food production, biological breeding for scientific animal research or horse breeding, which is highly regulated within the horse community. The Jackson Laboratories, in Bar Harbor, Maine, selectively breed mice for specific traits, depending on the experiment. Each year they supply over 2 million mice from more than 3,000 different strains to people in the research community. Some of these mice are bred for diabetes or neurology research. People who work in these types of breeding facilities must have specific degrees and training.

Horse breeding is a harder field to get into because of the high competition for positions. The community is a tight one and this is the type of field where you have to either know someone to get your foot in the door or pay your dues and hope you get in with the right people. You will need to gain hands-on experience and work with a breeder. Horse and farm animal breeders usually hire handlers to run their farms. There may only be one permanent handler on a farm, with the rest of the employees being seasonal or temporary. Handlers work for the owner and know how to work with the specific animal, feeding and vaccine requirements, housing and medical conditions.

If you choose to work in a breeding facility for research or zoos, you will most likely be working for a company like Pfizer or Abbott Labs, for the government or for a university, and be expected to follow regulations for that specific industry. Animal scientists need to be versed in genetics, nutrition, reproduction, growth and development of domestic farm animals. These jobs may include some office and some field work on a farm. People who work in these careers may advise farms on how to decrease animal mortality rates and develop proper husbandry practices. The job outlook in this area remains steady, although the job itself is shifting from how to get the most out of an animal to how to provide safe food for the public and humane living conditions for the animals.

Exotic breeding

Exotic animals are broadly defined as anything that is not a dog or a cat. Breeding exotic pocket pets such as geckos, snakes, rabbits or even hamsters is also becoming more popular. The USDA issues permits for keeping and breeding certain animals; in some cases, it may actually be illegal to transport certain animals into the United States. Exotic trade shows are held throughout the country, where breeders sell their animals along with proper food and cage set ups. If you do want to breed an exotic animal and are able to acquire the proper permit to keep an exotic species, you must then have proper housing, diet and a good working knowledge of that animal. You should also make sure there is a veterinarian available who is willing and able to help you in case a medical problem arises; some of these animals carry zoonotic diseases (those that people can catch) and you must be aware of, and if possible vaccinated against, those diseases.

Farming and Ranching

In farming and ranching, types of animals raised include horses, cows, sheep, goats, chickens, alpacas, pigs, rabbits and turkeys.

Family farms

Today, most family farms rely on the local community to sell their products. Not only are livestock raised, but land may be rented for other shared land use purposes such as growing a certain crop; additionally, equipment may be rented out. The "retirement" farm is gaining more favor with city and older people who may want to move to the country and/or leave their job. For those who want to relocate yet are not ready to give up working, it helps if you have a second career that you can do from a remote location to supplement your income, such as offering on-line accountant services during tax season. The benefit of this is that there are many government programs that help offset the cost of land if you are using it for farming purposes. The downside is that you must be up for the challenge of dealing with animals and their constant needs all year long.

Factory farms

In contrast is the large corporate factory farm, run by people located far away from the actual physical plant. Many family farms have been bought out by the larger corporate farms so that they now dominate the industry, thus leaving little room globally for these smaller farmers to sell their products. An example is Smithfield Foods Inc., now the largest pig and turkey producer in the U.S., which grew by acquiring other farm cooperatives and smaller corporations, some of which often included as many of 600,000 family farms. Large farms and producers have a lot of lobbying power in Washington and within the financial world, so they are often able to make government standards meet their needs. For example, it is widely believed that the waste produced by many of these farms causes illnesses in the communities where they are located, yet pollution laws are often swayed to favor these corporations.

Corporate factory farms are increasingly problematic. Many are mechanized and the animals have limited access to humans, grass or sun. They are often crippled and diseased, and in the worst cases can be unrecognizable under the filth in which they are forced to live. Feeding schedules are measured out and formulated with antibiotics to keep the stressed animals from succumbing to illness, and hormones are used to bulk them up. Jobs in these types of farms range from corporate-level, managing the economics of the business (which may rarely require stepping foot on a farm), to animal science, researching the best way to create the final "product" through reproduction and medications as economically efficiently as possible, to engineering, designing the farms and mechanized equipment used, to law, in many cases working to keep the farms out of litigation. Burnout can be high in a factory farming job, and in many cases a factory farm-related career means ignoring basic animal ethical standards. These jobs are not recommended for anyone who wants to promote animal welfare.

Next: cloning?

The U.S. Food and Drug Administration (FDA) is soon expected to release preliminary safety assessment that clears the way for marketing of meat and dairy products from cloned animals for human consumption. The assessment and the agency's expected endorsement of cloned food comes despite widespread concern among scientists and food safety advocates over the safety of such products.

Smaller farms and ranches

Working on smaller corporate, family or retirement farms or ranches allows the individual to get to know their stock. Animals are allowed a more natural existence, living in hay or roaming a field. This farm work requires the individual to spend long days outdoors facing all kinds of weather on a daily basis. Although it can be freeing to work outside, the work itself can be physically strenuous and requires skills that most people living in more urban areas do not develop. Ranchers are constantly moving herds or horses or cattle around and must learn to ride a horse. They must be comfortable camping out in the vast rangeland and must be able to respond incase a crisis evolves. If you are running a farm or ranch, a business sense is required as well in order to calculate daily and yearly expenses and to keep track of your gains and losses.

Most small farms and ranches are run by family members and, depending on the size, one or two outside workers. Outside help may be hired if the season and extra work dictates. Retirement farmers may take on the work themselves, depending on the number of livestock they keep, calling out for services such as veterinary or for equipment repairs.

Most of these farms cater to their local community and use their livestock for what they produce (eggs or milk). Many of them also give tours of their facilities and emphasize their food products as a reconnection with nature instead of a way to refuel quickly. DanaRay farm in Branchville, New Jersey, is a small community farm that promotes healthy living and education about naturally farmed products. They sell pasture-raised chickens and hen eggs, naturally fed pigs and they use their goats' milk to produce other products. They also grow produce and cut flowers depending on the season. The Glaum Egg Farm in California has been struggling to remain a family business, and combats the large corporations by filling a niche in raising cage-free Certified Humane Raised and Handled eggs as well as organic eggs. They have also grown beyond their community, selling to restaurants, local stores and customers direct from the site.

Jamison Farm in Pennsylvania began as a hobby (the owners raised sheep) and is now a business that raises 5,000 sheep a year on over 200 acres.

The day-to-day

This might all seem charmingly bucolic, but on a small farm or ranch, there is work to do from sunrise to sunset, seven days a week. When working with live animals, there can be emergencies at any time of day, and there is little or no time for vacation, as the animals must be cared for continually. Daily operation of the financial and office part of the business must be balanced with caring for the animals, upkeep of the facilities and machinery. Farm or ranch owners also need to keep up with the latest trends and government regulations by attending local meetings, national conferences, subscribing to journals and checking online information. Farming and ranching jobs are for people who are ready to live and breathe their everyday trials along with their joys. This job will become your way of life.

Animal Control Officers/Public Safety

Animal control programs are usually government-funded public resources, though some are private nonprofits, providing places to bring homeless animals and outlets for the reporting of abuse cases for investigation. They also pick up stray animals, protect the public from possible dangerous wild animal attacks and provide education and basic vaccination and spay neuter programs for the public.

Animal shelters

Shelters with animal control programs cater to different needs, depending on the area of the country they're in. Urban communities might not tolerate a nuisance bear as a country town might! Shelters are required to keep their facilities clean and free of disease, and they must maintain regular feeding and exercise schedules and include medical treatment (preventative measures such as spaying/neutering and vaccines) for the animals they house. The animals should be groomed and socialized where reasonable. Cleaning bowls, doing laundry and restocking supplies are other tasks that need to be done.

Shelters need to staff appropriately to care for the number of animals they keep, and depend on a large number of professionals and volunteers to run smoothly. This includes animal control officers, dog trainers, veterinarians, technicians, kennel workers and shelter administration. The director of the facility, aside from running the shelter, makes sure all laws are being adhered to. Certified animal control officers are out in the field, whereas animal care workers (mostly volunteer) take care of the animals once they are at the facility. Veterinary technicians and/or veterinarians are often on site at larger shelters to deal with the animals' medical needs. Animal behaviorists and trainers may also be on site to work with animals and prospective adoptive families; larger municipal shelters housing a few hundred animals, such as the ASPCA shelters in many cities across the country, may employee people with experience in psychology who would work with the dog trainers and other staff when screening people as potential new owners for animals. There may be various desk jobs available where computer knowledge or promotional skills are needed.

Not all fun and games

If you choose to volunteer or work in the kennel area with the animals, you must be prepared not only physically, but also mentally for the challenges you will face. There may be animals who do not find homes or who are too sick to rehabilitate and require euthanasia. You may put your own heath at risk by coming into contact with diseases that can be transmitted to humans or by exposing yourself to aggressive animals that may bite or scratch. You may be required to be vaccinated for rabies as a preventative measure. The hours are long and the pay is low.

Working in animal control will put you in contact with the public where you will be required to handle difficult emotional situations in a calm, dignified manner. Your hours may be comprised of various shift work to accommodate around-the-clock hours, especially if the shelter is short-staffed. But the work is definitely not boring. Each new situation requires quick, safe problem-solving. Most people in animal control jobs are in it for the fast-paced, emergency-type vibe that can be present when going on cases. You may come across fractious animals, angry, upset or irresponsible pet owners, or a boxful of hungry kittens. You may be sent to pick up road kill or handle potentially rabid wild animals.

Both animal control and shelter work handle issues of public health safety and deal with the law pertaining to animals. This type of work can be as dangerous and frustrating as it is rewarding, knowing that you made a difference to one life.

Petfinder.com, a web site dedicated to finding lost pets, links to shelters and rescue groups all over the United States and acts as a unifying database.

Veterinary Technician

Today veterinary technicians play a role akin to that of a nurse, with skills and education to match. Working under the supervision of a licensed veterinarian, the veterinary technician has a dynamic job with many different roles to take on—from working in private practice to diagnostic laboratories, humane societies, zoos, teaching, biomedical research or sales.

Veterinary technicians also work in hospital environments, ranging from one-doctor clinics to 40-doctor specialty practices to large university teaching hospitals. Wildlife rescue facilities and farm animals also need veterinary technicians. Some technicians may take on teaching jobs in college veterinary technology programs, lecture at national conferences or write articles for trade magazines, and some gain further training in management to become hospital administrators.

Veterinarian technician responsibilities

Day-to-day circumstances change constantly for a vet tech depending on the patients presenting to the clinic, and duties performed usually depend on the schedule of the doctor for the day. Daily duties range from client education, laboratory work, doing inventory, taking radiographs, performing dental procedures, troubleshooting equipment, placing IV catheters and taking blood samples, preparing patients for surgery, giving life-support to critically ill patients and so on. But an emergency situation can always present itself. Technicians are relied on to be flexible, good communicators and well-versed in all areas. They are able to assist in many of the aspects of the hospital, but they are not legally allowed to diagnose, perform surgery, or prescribe medication. A job in this field often requires long hours at work, sometimes on weekends, overnights or holidays. Technicians are often called upon to organize the day, hire and train entry level staff and set an example for the rest of the support staff.

Specialties

Veterinary technician specialties are growing as the demand for veterinarian specialties grows. According to the U.S. Department of Labor, this field is burgeoning, with more experienced and educated veterinary technicians replacing more entry-level assistants. The Academy of Veterinary Emergency and Critical Care Technician specialty group, one of the first such specialty groups to be formed, continues to set standards for subsequent technician specialties. Within the veterinary technician community generally, there is a strong network and support system, and many organizations exist on local as well as state levels. The largest group in the United States for veterinary technicians is the National Association of Veterinary Technicians of America (NAVTA). This organization offers various resources aiding in the continued professional growth of its members.

Zookeeper and Wildlife Management

Zookeepers spend their days cleaning and repairing cages and enclosures, preparing meticulously formulated diets and feeding it to the animals safely, raising young animals, and, overall, monitoring the animals under their care. They must record their observations, keeping watch for signs of sickness, changes in eating patterns or behavior, as well as any repair needs of the enclosures. Under the supervision of a veterinarian, keepers may be required to give medications or basic treatments, administer vaccines, and assist in surgical or other procedures.

Zookeepers may give tours to the public and should be able to answer questions about the animals they work with, which requires not only depth of knowledge but strong public speaking skills. Because of the physical demands of the job, zookeepers must also be in good shape.

Veterinarians who work in zoos or wildlife facilities first gain experience in small animal medicine. Working in a zoo or wildlife facility requires specific knowledge about the animals you will be handling and treating.

Curators

Zoo curators oversee the types of animals, amount of animals and care of animals in the zoo. They work closely with the zoo directors, who are responsible for the administrative duties of the facility.

Curators are involved in creating a budget to create and carry out goals for the zoo they work for, such as designing educational programs for the public or breeding plans for the animals. These are the people who delegate to the staff, making sure that everything runs smoothly. They are also involved in zoo loaning and breeding programs with other zoos and transportation of properly prepared deceased animals to museums for display. Curators often write articles for journals and may fill out applications for grants.

Wildlife education and rehab

Some zoologists focus on animal and wildlife education. They may be involved in creating zoo programs and educational material for the public. They may also give guided tours or set up exhibits in parks or museums.

Wildlife rehabilitators care for sick, injured or orphaned wildlife. Once the animal is ready to be on its own, it is released back into its natural habitat. Rehabilitators, who must be trained, need to have permits from the state they are working in or from a federal wildlife agency to handle wildlife. Areas of rehabilitation may include dealing with injuries sustained from hunting and trapping, logging activity or oil spills. Other jobs in this area may be found in state or federal parks, where important duties include monitoring the wildlife population, maintaining trails and overseeing population control or restocking ponds for fishing, regulating hunting guidelines and dealing with nuisance animals in camping areas.

Two well-known zoos that are very active in the wildlife conservation arena are The National Zoo in Washington, D.C. and the Bronx Zoo in New York City.

Zoologists

Zoologists and wildlife biologists are similar in that they both study animals in the wild. They may take on research to study the origin, behavior, illnesses and overall way of life of the animals they are studying. Information is gathered on populations of animals or specific measurements of individuals in their natural settings or a more controlled one—which may include sedating and trapping animals to gather the information. When out in the field, zoologists log long hours observing their subjects and making notes. Back in the office, the information must be correlated and made into written form. In conducting research on an animal's environment and how use of land affects how they are living there, data collected can help in protecting a particular area where an animal is becoming extinct. Some zoologists perform necropsies after an animal has died to gather information about their organs and structure.

Categories of zoologists include those who study mammals (mammalogists), birds (ornithologists), reptiles (herpetologists) and fish (ichthyologists). Because the world's wild places are rapidly disappearing, the study of animals in their natural setting helps raise awareness of how the world's increasing human population is infringing on that of animals. These jobs are best suited to a creative, hardy, unique individual who enjoys being outdoors in any kind of weather. Some aspects of the direct work may be dangerous, such as when administering medicine or doing field work.

Biology and Research

Biological scientist jobs involve the study of living organisms and how they relate to their environment, and may involve more specialized work in zoology or microbiology. Most work is done in a laboratory setting, and funding for projects may come from private sources, government-sponsored programs or through grants. This research becomes fundamental to much of the progress made in areas such as medicine, environmental concerns and the food industry.

Work environment

Although many people enter the biological sciences or laboratory field with the intent of working independently, employees still need to be able to work as part of a team and need to have strong communication skills, both verbal and written. Patience, focus and integrity are needed to follow through with precise experimental data and to stick with long, sometimes repetitive experiments, whether on genetics or crop production. Although laboratory jobs are relatively safe, some working conditions may expose employees to toxic substances or organisms that may be dangerous, so proper knowledge of handling these materials and of safety procedures is essential. Obviously, lab workers must be comfortable using and troubleshooting laboratory equipment, as well as knowledge of the handling and care of laboratory animals or plants.

Specialties

Areas of specialty within these fields include marine biology (marine biologists study the organisms in that live in the ocean), zoology (the study of animal life in a natural setting, most often associated with zoos), biochemistry (the study of systems in a laboratory setting), botany (study of plant science which can be associated with animal habitats), and ecology (study of the relationship between living things and the environment).

There are also jobs related to agriculture and food science such as farming, food research and genetics of food animals.

Administrative positions in this kind of research require a strong business background as well as knowledge of the regulatory issues pertaining to the relevant industry.

Pet Service Industries

Jobs in these fields, which include kennels, retail pet stores and grooming, vary according to the business. Small businesses may offer only grooming services or kennel services, but larger corporations and chain stores such as PetSmart hire a variety of people to offer a range of services that may include basic veterinary care, dog training and grooming along with selling pet supplies. Working for a larger chain pet store provides a steady stream of clients. These stores may also work with local shelters, showing animals who need homes on special "adoption days" at the store. If you are business-oriented and are prepared to put a lot of work into a business, you can create your own niche. A pet store can deal exclusively in one type of animal, such as fish, while also offering home aquarium services, for example.

Entry level jobs in these fields, where turnover is high, can offer flexibility for first time workers in the industry.

Petsitting and dogwalking

These kinds of jobs are primarily filled by people who need to work with animals, but who do not wish to go through further formal education or work in a medical setting. Still, these jobs can be physically demanding, emotionally exhausting and in some cases, dangerous.

A petsitter should be prepared to be available at all hours of the day and night. You can limit your jobs to specific days and hours, but if you want to make money, demand for your services will be heaviest on weekends and holidays, and you will be needed to check on pets early in the morning and late at night. Depending on the needs of the pets and clients, each visit will take at least 45 minutes (not including transportation time to and from the job). You should give yourself time to socialize with the pet, do any necessary walks or feedings, give any needed medications and clean up after yourself. You constantly need to be prepared for the unexpected events that could add time onto each visit. People are trusting you with their pets and homes, so showing that you are up to the responsibility is essential. Some petsitters may take the pets into their homes, which cuts out the traveling time. But there will be a limit as to how many animals you can take on at one time, and you must always provide a safe environment for the pets you are watching. There may also be local laws in your town limiting you as to the number of animals you can keep in your residence at one time.

Dog walking requires less of a time commitment and most services areneeded at lunchtime during the day or an occasional weekend to break up the day when an owner is out for long periods of time. There may also be owners who are home but cannot take their dogs out for long walks because of medical problems or another reason. Some of these jobs may include giving medications or just checking on a pet that may not be well.

Kennels

You may want to take your pet watching services further and work in or open a kennel. Kennel work involves varied hours that include weekends, holidays, early mornings and early evenings. Summers and holidays are busy times. Kennels hold a larger number of pets, and each needs individual attention. Some kennels offer periods of socialization during the day, which means the animals require supervision while in a group setting. Working in a kennel assumes knowledge of animal behavior as well as patience and the ability to anticipate problems. You will need to recognize signs of illness and act quickly to ensure the health of the ailing pet as well as shield the other boarders from any infectious diseases. Depending on what your kennel job is, you may need to know about the medical conditions of the pets you take in, as well as any vaccinations required. More and more people are seeking out day care for their dogs, dropping them off in the morning before work and picking them up on the way home. These facilities offer socialization to the dogs while their owners are at work (as well as eliminating the guilt felt by the owner from leaving their pet home alone all day). Many kennels require grooming knowledge as many include these services in their boarding price.

Larger kennels are increasingly prevalent in heavily populated areas, offering basic animal care, socialization and grooming. These businesses may also have animal behaviorists on staff who can help other workers with socialization of animals. A given business may also be affiliated with a local veterinarian.

Pet stores/retail

Working in a pet store is similar to working in any retail job, but in this case you need to be well versed in pet products and care to help customers. You may work days, weekends or evenings. Store managers are responsible for ordering supplies, hiring and firing staff and providing basic training for the staff. They deal with any problems that arise during the day and make sure the stores are running smoothly. If the pet store sells live animals (and not just supplies) someone will need to be responsible for caring for the animals before they are sold. This includes recognizing signs of illness and seeking medical care for any animals needing it.

Although many pet stores now rent out part of their store to businesses offering grooming services, basic veterinary care and to shelters offering animals for adoption, there are still pet stores that sell puppies, kittens, rabbits, birds and other pets without the proper staff to meet the needs of these animals while they are in the store's care. As people continue to seek out more exotic pets, knowledgeable pet store staff is increasingly necessary.

Grooming

Entry-level grooming jobs usually include bathing and drying the animals. As basic skill level increases, other tasks include brushing out, final clipping or shaving, nail clipping and ear cleaning. Groomers often work shorter hours or base their hours on scheduled appointments. Holidays and summer can be busier, as pets may need more extreme haircuts or baths from increased activity level. Both dogs and cats go to groomers, so those in this field must understand how to handle both. Most pets are not cooperative in this context, so groomers must learn specific techniques for restraining animals while bathing, clipping, and drying them. Patience and a calm demeanor also help. There is a growing demand for groomers who make house calls, either in the client's house or in specially equipped vans. Attending trade shows and networking with other groomers can be valuable in helping to start or expand a successful grooming business.

Corporate/Government Jobs

Corporate jobs involving animals may include working for a pharmaceutical company as a representative, researcher or animal technician. You may work for a private business such as a zoo or pet store. Different departments within an animal facility can include human resources, legal affairs or marketing. More and more private animal hospitals are being established, with some chain animal hospitals, such as those owned by Banfield with over 500 locations nationwide, employing people on levels ranging from upper management to accounting to doctors and technicians. Shows such as *Animal Planet* employ people to develop show content or do promotional work.

Government jobs (federal, state and local) include working in research and testing laboratories, such as the National Institutes of Health, zoos such as the Smithsonian or inspecting animal facilities with agencies like the USDA. Other positions may include teaching in state-owned universities.

Major Employers

CHAPTER 4

In this chapter, we'll take a look at the various places you might be working in a career with animals.

Breeding Facilities

Breeding facilities vary from well-regulated corporate structures that breed for research and employ college-educated staff to the independent breeder who sells to the person on the street. There are captive breeding programs within zoos and breeding programs on horse farms, both of which require experience, and in the case of zoos, a college education (BS). Many factory-farmed animals, horses and even dogs are now bred via artificial insemination because they may not be able to breed normally any longer (a result, in some cases, of the way this process has altered animals physically). Artificial insemination can also be used if the mating pair live a far distance from each other, or if the breeder needs/wants to have more control over the gene pool. In these cases, veterinarians or other professionals should be enlisted for help, because specific techniques and monitoring equipment is necessary to carry this out properly.

Before turning a breeding hobby into a home business, you should research and make sure there is a need for the animal you are breeding. There are too many unwanted animals in the world, and one more uneducated breeder only adds to the problem.

Corporate and Independent Farms

Large corporate farms dominate the industry, but their practices may be unethical, and you should thoroughly do your research before signing on to work in such a place. One of the country's largest poultry slaughterhouses, North Carolina's House of Raeford Farms, Inc., was secretly investigated in 2007. The USDA was shown the tapes of turkeys being abused, and an advisor commented on the poor management of the facility.

Many smaller farms throughout the country treat animals humanely, and take pride in what they do. An internet search is a good way to find farms in your area. Sites like http://www.smallfarmsuccess.info/index.cfm offer resources if you want to start your own small, sustainable farm, and some states, such as New Jersey and New York, have university co-operative extensions that provide information.

Animal Shelters

Animal shelters exist in communities across the U.S. and employ animal control officers, kennel workers and trainers. Shelter directors are usually veterinarians and/or have extensive experience in the field of management. Technicians monitor the day-to-day care of the animals, with the aid of a veterinarian a phone call away if needed. Public relations is becoming a larger part of the animal shelter dynamic, with events being planned to raise money for the shelters, or to increase awareness of animals needing homes. Foster homes are sometimes needed when a shelter cannot house animals with specific needs, such as newborn kittens needing bottle feeding round the clock.

Organizations such as the ASPCA (The American Society for the Prevention of Cruelty to Animals) work toward promoting increased care for animals in shelters. They also promote proper care of pets and help to develop programs for the public to assist in education and funding for these issues. They work with local police officers in training them to help combat cruelty to animals. More recently, the ASPCA has created a Pet Health Insurance available for public purchase. The ASPCA also acts as an advocate in the passage of bills that promote standards for the treatment of all animals. Some of the laws created under these bills include making it a crime to leave pets unattended in vehicles in dangerous conditions, ensuring that animal safety and rescue is a part of a community's emergency preparedness program and measures for animal population control via increased funding for sterilization.

The Humane Society of the United States is the largest animal welfare organization in the world. Although it does not regulate animal shelters, it acts as a resource for them, making recommendations and providing information. It also provides assistance to advocates for animal rights.

Hospitals

Facilities range from one-person clinics to 40-person operations, and services offered can fluctuate too. The Animal Medical Center in New York City hires hundreds of people, offering a wide range of services 24 hours a day. National, corporate-owned hospitals such as Banfield may only offer basic preventative and support care during working hours. There are hospitals within some zoo facilities, and some veterinary colleges such as UC Davis have a teaching hospital open to the public where pre-veterinary students train under staff supervision.

Hospitals employ professionals in a number of roles. Veterinarians are the licensed doctors who examine patients and devise respective medical plans. Credentialed veterinary technicians are often on staff, particularly in larger facilities, or in states requiring the presence of credentialed veterinary technicians when performing specific tasks such as inducing anesthesia. Other support staff include assistants, kennel workers, receptionists, administration and management, marketing, and building maintenance. Smaller facilities may combine these jobs into one role, whereas larger hospitals may break them down into different jobs.

Veterinary hospital

Jobs within an animal hospital include veterinarians and a support staff. The volume of support staff usually correlates to the number of veterinarians on staff, but can be broken down into the following. Animal care workers are needed to feed, walk and keep patients clean. Technicians assist doctors with medical procedures. Office staff facilitates client procedures and paperwork, and hospital administration aids hospital staff.

In large university settings, like the aforementioned University of California Davis School of Veterinary Medicine, there is a huge quantity of departments, so the college serves as a resource for the veterinary community as well as the public. Its veterinary program addresses animals as well as public and environmental health; the staff includes veterinarians, researchers and laboratory support staff, technicians and administration along with the teachers and students. In the campus hospital, students gain both academic and hands-on experience on real patients.

UC Davis's vet school is a teaching hospital, which means it uses the most current equipment and medicine and staffs high-level, certified veterinarians and technicians to help facilitate learning in a real hospital setting. Most of the staff are teachers as well as workers, and must be at the top of their field to be able to lecture and teach.

Veterinary Facility Snapshot

Oradell Animal Hospital, Inc.
Paramus, NJ
Clinical Excellence, Compassionate Care, Exceptional Service
www.oradell.com

The Oradell Animal Hospital is one of the country's largest privately owned companion animal veterinary hospitals. The hospital runs 24 hours a day, seven days a week, 365 days a year and offers specialty medicine and emergency services for dogs, cats and exotic pets day and night. Oradell's reputation extends across the country, as it sets the standard for how a privately owned animal hospital can service the community.

History

The hospital was established in 1961 by Dr. Gary Johnson and Dr. Anthony Palminteri. These two newly graduated veterinarians completed internships and started their practice in a small house. Trading shifts to cover emergencies around the clock, they continued to expand the practice, taking on a third partner, Dr. William Stockman, in 1967, and eventually growing to a staff of eight. In 2000, the hospital had outgrown its physical space with over 30 staff doctors and 150 support staff on the payroll. A new hospital now includes 36,000 square feet to provide for each of the department specialties, 22 exam rooms and office space. Two smaller clinics, which serve as outpatient facilities for the community, are owned and staffed by the Oradell Animal Hospital.

Hospital management

Responsibilities break down as follows. The hospital is overseen by a board of directors. Managers, with the help of their supervisors, run each department and each outpatient clinic. Human Resources manages most matters pertaining to employees such as recruitment, orientation, contract preparation and employee benefits. The hospital controller is responsible for the keeping of all financial records associated with the corporation and its business, including receipts, disbursements, general ledger, cash management and payroll. The hospital administrator works closely with the hospital director and assistant director to handle all billing and client-related financial matters. The director of staff development and client communications mentors staff members on supervisory and leadership skills and oversees the client services, purchasing and marketing departments. Staff development and client communications also works with local veterinarians to ensure smooth processes when referring clients to the hospital. The marketing and public relations coordinator's responsibilities include web site design and maintenance, design and distribution of printed materials, public relations and communications. The purchasing agent's job is to purchase all equipment and supplies for the hospital and its satellite clinics. He is responsible for maintaining all hospital inventories, selecting and maintaining efficient sources of supply and creating good relationships with vendors. His staff assists with the receiving, stocking, distribution and security of equipment and supplies purchased for hospital use.

At the front desk, clients are greeted by members of the client services department. This department encompasses greeters, room fillers, phone operators, medical record clerks, chart reviewers and cashiers and is led by a manager and five supervisors.

Clinic Services

The clinic services department, headed by a manager with three supervisors, includes the pharmacy, laboratory and exam room assistants. The pharmacy and laboratory are staffed seven days a week, day and evening, and experience here varies—you'll find entry-level assistants as well as credentialed veterinary technicians and certified laboratory personnel. But all clinical services staff is required to know basic animal restraint and is trained to assist doctors in medical exams and in providing basic laboratory tests. These tests are performed by the in-house lab staff, which also prepares samples to be sent to an outside laboratory facility. As results come back, they are placed in the patient's chart for doctor review. Pharmacy personnel must be familiar with the medications dispensed and be able to council clients in administration of the medications. The hospital runs its own blood banking through this department, using employees' pets as donors to supplement blood supplies purchased from outside vendors.

Animal ER

The emergency and in-patient care services department is handled by a manager and five supervisors. This department also runs 24 hours a day, seven days a week and must be staffed and trained accordingly. A doctor board-certified in emergency and critical care helps coordinate the department along with two credentialed technicians who are also specialists certified in emergency and critical care. ECC doctors, credentialed technicians and assistants are experienced in triage and critical care medicine as well as routine patient care; all emergencies are triaged by a technician before patients see a doctor. This department sets the protocols for the overall care of in-hospital patients and how medication and treatments are given. After-hour emergency services include radiology, surgery, ultrasound and endoscopy.

Patient services

The patient services department, run by a manager and two supervisors, includes the technical support staff of various specialized services including surgery, medicine, cardiology, radiology & MRI and physical rehabilitation. This department is responsible for hiring, training and scheduling all the support staff for these various services. Each service has a credentialed, experienced veterinary technician assisting the veterinary specialist; technicians may liaise with clients, assist the doctor with any diagnostic testing that may be performed, and help in scheduling appointments. Technicians must also communicate and coordinate with other departments when other services are needed.

Radiology

In the radiology department, veterinary technicians also perform MRIs and are well versed in running all of the imaging equipment. Surgery technicians, who prepare patients for surgery, are experienced and knowledgeable about sedation and anesthesia. They must know how to work anesthesia machines and blood pressure units and be able to recognize changes in patient status while under anesthesia. The surgery department has an after-hours on-call schedule that ensures a surgeon and technician are available after hours if emergency surgery is needed. The internal medicine and cardiology departments run ultrasound and endoscopic tests on patients and offer these diagnostic in-house services to referrals from area hospitals. Physical rehabilitation is run by a staff doctor certified in canine rehabilitation and another staff surgeon who practices acupuncture. An assistant helps in scheduling appointments for the service and takes in patients for the day following the rehabilitation protocols prescribed by the doctor. Depending on the type of rehabilitation needed, the patients may receive therapeutic exercise or ultrasound stimulation or they may spend time on the underwater treadmill. The hospital also offers nutritional counseling, behavior, dermatology and bereavement sessions.

Employee programs

The hospital has an internship program for veterinarians; 12 interns are admitted to the program through a national match program. The program is 13 months long, during which interns rotate through all departments. Other hospital programs include those for veterinary student externs who may visit for two weeks at a time. Veterinary technician externships are also offered for students needing to complete requirements for graduation. Continuing education lectures are offered monthly for the support staff, with lunchtime rounds during the week for the veterinary staff. Continuing education is also offered for area veterinarians and clients, with monthly programs available.

Benefits offered for support and veterinary staff include paid time off, including holiday, sick time, vacations and night differentials for working off-hours, medical health benefits, long-term profit sharing, a savings bond program, paid uniform allowance, continuing education allowance programs, medical health benefits for pets and in-house continuing education along with continual on-the-job training.

As pet ownership continues to increase, the hospital has become a valuable resource for other area animal hospitals and shelters because of the specialty services it provides.

Laboratories

Many employers in the pharmaceutical arena look for high-level employees at the top of their respective field (veterinary or technician.) These labs, such as those at Pfizer and Abbott, employ people to work in their animal division. That division includes sales jobs, in which employees travel to different facilities and work with staff to learn new equipment or teach about a new drug to be introduced. Those who work in the labs themselves, performing experiments and monitoring animals, may have more stable Monday through Friday jobs. Lab work can require both assistants and technicians to carry out the work, with a researcher in charge. Vets and technicians are on hand to make sure the animals under their care are comfortable and that there are regular inspections of the facilities.

Zoos

Zoos require that a veterinarian be on staff, with most large places hiring their own in-house veterinarian and smaller facilities having one on-call. Larger facilities will take veterinarians as part of a residency program. It is the job of these caretakers to make sure the zoo animals are properly cared for. Other employees are hired with previous experience, and usually with a B.S. degree or veterinary technology certification. There may be other helpers who volunteer their time educating the public about the animals in the zoo. Zoo staff also typically includes a director and an office staff.

Some major zoos and aquariums around the country include the San Diego Zoo (CA), the Bronx Zoo (NY), Sea World/Busch Gardens (FL), Mystic Seaport (CT), and the Nashville Zoo and Wildlife Park.

Schools

Many colleges with agricultural or animal science programs employee veterinarians as part of their teaching staff. In some cases, these employees work full-time for the college, acting as advisors to students as well as teachers. In states that have land grants, these professors may also work in research. Rutgers University in New Jersey is one such college, where the faculty not only lectures and advises, but also works with agricultural and medical businesses to help carry out research for the industry. Students are then used to help carry out the research either as part of their education programs or as part-time jobs while in school. If a college does have research facilities, it also hires a staff with at least a B.S. to help run the laboratory.

Veterinary technician colleges employ credentialed technicians to teach classes. Usually, a veterinarian directs the program, working with a technician who helps organize the curriculum. These teaching jobs may be full- or part-time. There are several long distance technician programs that require staff to run the programs. These include courses offered by Purdue University and Penn Foster.

Conferences

Conferences abound within the veterinary, laboratory, farm animal and related fields, and are held nationwide. Lecturers are usually paid per lecture and are given a stipend to cover travel and room expenses. The American Animal Hospital Association hosts one national yearly conference; almost 4,000 professionals attend for over 280 hours of continuing education covering scientific, management, technician and team topics.

CAREERS

GETTING HIRED

VETERINARY AND ANIMAL CAREERS

Education

CHAPTER 5

In this chapter, we'll lay out basic information about education and training needed for the various animal career fields. More detailed information on specific jobs can be found within each corresponding chapter later in the guide. Keep in mind that a career working with animals means dedicating yourself to a lifelong journey of continual learning and experience. There are many sources of information at your disposal: magazines, books, journals, web sites, certificate programs, associations, seminars and conferences are all ways to learn about a particular career path.

Getting Started: Associate's or Bachelor's Degree

Associate's or Bachelor's degrees in Animal Science or similar studies, such as biology, are required for most jobs within the animal fields, including zoology, research, animal science, food production, and pre-veterinary. Biological science majors are included in most college curriculums. If you are undecided on a career track, it may be best to choose biology as a major, as most of the math and science classes within this major can be applied to many types of jobs. Colleges with land grants, like Rutgers and Cornell, have strong animal sciences programs, which are helpful for farming, research or pre-veterinary tracks. Land grant schools (state universities) and colleges in rural communities tend to be strong in agricultural courses, and often these schools offer wildlife and zoo management degrees. You can find out the availability of these programs by contacting a school directly or researching it online.

Becoming a Veterinarian

Becoming a veterinarian used to be the first career option people would think of when considering working with animals. (Because there are now so many other choices for working with animals, becoming a veterinarian is not necessarily the main option any longer.) Regardless, thinking about becoming a veterinarian should preferably begin as early as high school, especially for students who excel in math and science. Because veterinary school requires so much time and expense—encompassing both college and then veterinary school—you should first gain experience by volunteering in a veterinary hospital or other facility just to make sure it's the right career path for you. Many people decide, after gaining employment in some type of animal career, that the time and money spent on becoming a veterinarian is not the option they were looking for.

Early preparation

Starting in high school, math, science and biology classes are needed to enter a college animal science or equivalent bachelor program. To be considered a viable candidate for admissions to a college with a pre-veterinary track, your grades must be high. Other factors admissions boards will weigh are the types of electives you have taken, volunteer hours, any jobs you may have had while in high school and sports you may have played. Although most of these things should reflect an interest in working with animals, admissions officers are looking for a well-rounded person who has a drive to succeed. Letters of recommendation should reflect these elements of your personality as well as your interest in the field of veterinary medicine.

Pre-veterinary or equivalent college course requirements include classes in math (usually calculus), biology, organic chemistry, physics, nutrition, microbiology and physiology along with typical core classes such as English and humanities. Again, you should round out your college academics with other activities showing your interest in veterinary medicine. Joining pre-veterinary clubs, volunteering on the college farm, participating in local animal groups and working in a veterinary clinic are all typical extracurricular activities that pre-veterinary majors list on their veterinary applications.

Unconventional paths

If you do not choose a pre-veterinary course of study, you should research what specific courses are required to be admitted to veterinary school and make sure you fit them into your course of study. You could potentially be an English major in college with a minor in Biology; as long as you have all of the prerequisites for admission to veterinary school, you can apply. It may also be wise to phone in to a veterinary college and inquire about the respective admission board's view of taking this alternate. If possible, you should continue to work and gain experience in a veterinary hospital while attending school or during breaks.

Veterinary school

After obtaining a four-year degree or equivalent college credits, veterinary school applicants must sit for the Graduate Record Examination (GRE). Some veterinary colleges also require scores from the Veterinary College of Admission Test (VCAT) or the Medical College Admission Test (MCAT) before you can apply to their school. Although an undergraduate degree is not necessary to apply to veterinary school, given the competition for places it can be almost impossible to be admitted without it.

Where to find a veterinary college

There are only 28 veterinary colleges in the U.S., the oldest of which is at Iowa State. Elsewhere, Cornell has been an academic leader since 1894 not only for its veterinary medicine program, but also its biomedical research and public health programs. Most American veterinary programs usually only admit students who reside in their state. States without veterinary schools may have specific contracts set up with states that do have them (called "contract schools"), but only a limited number of these spots for out-of-state applicants are available. So the competition to get into veterinary school is high and you need to have the best grades and test scores possible to increase your chances of getting in.

If you do not live in a state with a veterinary college, you may need to relocate before applying to establish your residence in the state of choice. Many applicants also opt to do their undergraduate degree at a school that has an established veterinary college, thus increasing their chances of being accepted to a veterinary program. If you are starting later in life with this career path, you may have an advantage over younger applicants, because admission boards are always looking out for someone whose profile stands out, and they also like to see people who have a strong desire to work in the field. Another factor that may increase your admittance to veterinary school is hands-on experience in a private or institutionalized veterinary setting. Volunteer work in a shelter or for a breeder may also help put you above applicants who have little or no experience. It is a good idea to start looking into requirements of the veterinary schools you are interested in before graduating from college.

Some schools outside the U.S. take American residents and are worth looking into. One of these programs is Ross University, established in 1982 on the island of St. Kitts. Some foreign veterinary schools have contracts with U.S. schools to take the top percentage of their students during their final year, thereby allowing them graduation from the U.S. college. For those who graduate from veterinary colleges outside of the U.S., an exam given by the National Board of Veterinary Medical Examiners (NBVME) must be taken to apply for a veterinary license.

Internships

Many veterinarians enter into yearlong internships after finishing veterinary school. These programs are available across the country, often at large veterinary facilities that offer 24-hour care and have a variety of specialists on staff; applicants are chosen through a nationwide match system. The benefit is intense, constant on-the-job training from experienced specialists in the field, and veterinarians who complete this yearlong internship before entering into regular practice are typically better prepared to deal with a larger range of cases early in their careers. Interns also often have a bigger pool of higher paying positions to choose from because of their higher level of experience. Many larger hospitals, both private and university, will only hire applicants with this extra training.

Internship programs are often stressful mentally and physically; they require long hours at any time of day or night, without much pay in part due to the grueling hours; externships may offer a better work schedule depending on the specialty.

Residency

After completing an internship year, a veterinarian is eligible to apply for a residency [externship] for a specialty. Specialty externships usually last three or four years and offer more intense training in a certain area of medicine, such as surgery, internal medicine, or emergency and critical care. These positions can be difficult to obtain, though, and completing an internship along with strong letters of recommendations can help secure a position. Applicants who still have a hard time gaining an externship may choose to take on another internship or similar job geared toward desired experience to boost externship candidacy.

Certification

After completing an externship program, the veterinarian is eligible to sit for a certifying exam in their field of specialty. Those who attain certification are called board certified specialists and, as in human medicine, include specialties such as medicine, surgery, radiology, emergency and critical care, and physical therapy. Veterinarians who pass the exam and become board certified in a specialty are sought out by larger practices such as universities and teaching hospitals, but private practices are increasingly seeking out these specialists as pet owners demand better and more sophisticated care for their pets.

Licensing and continuing education

Graduation from a veterinary college with a DVM or VMD degree and licensing by the state you are working in is required to be a practicing veterinarian. Exams vary state to state, but you must pass a state licensing exam to practice.

Most states require veterinarians to fulfill a certain number of continuing education credits each year while they are practicing to ensure they are up to date on the most recent medical findings. There are many journals and clubs, local, national and global, catering to the veterinary field. Conferences are held year round, worldwide, where veterinarians get up-to-date information and network with others in their field. Conferences also provide the opportunity to meet with vendors and learn about new industry products. Online sources also offer a way to meet continued education credits; in addition, extensive online databases allow veterinarians to research cases as they present themselves.

Vet school demographics

In the beginning, veterinarians were primarily male. Today, though only 30 percent of practicing veterinarians are women, over 70 percent of students enrolled in veterinary colleges are female. Many veterinary schools are looking for male applicants to balance their student population. Roles within the workplace are also balancing the male to female ratio. More woman veterinarians are gaining specialty certifications, making a place for themselves in this growing industry.

Veterinary Technicians

Veterinary technical programs

Credentialed veterinary technicians have taken and passed the National Veterinary Technician Exam. They may have college degrees (AS or BS) in animal science, but as of 2007 must have graduated from an accredited veterinary technician program to sit for the exam. Once this certification is in hand, people in this field may choose to become certified in areas such as ECC (emergency and critical care), anesthesiology, internal medicine or dentistry. It usually takes a minimum of 3 years to meet all requirements to sit for the specialty exam. Other technicians may specialize "unofficially" as they find a certain niche within their job—like lab work, physical rehab, oncology or working in management.

Veterinary technology programs offer either two-year associates' or four-year bachelor's of science degrees specifically in this field, although the BS degree in veterinary technology is often harder to find as a program. (Delhi College in New York, for one, offers this degree.) Veterinary technical programs within a college must be accredited by the AAHA for its students to be eligible to sit for the National Veterinary Technician Exam (NVTE).

Community colleges may offer a two-year associates degree in veterinary technology, which will at least set you up for an entry-level position in this career. Most classes focus on science and laboratory procedures, with some hands on training offered during externships. Externships are usually required as part of the degree process and they vary by school. Four-year bachelor's degrees offer more of an educational background in medicine along with the laboratory procedures and hands-on training. Obviously, technicians graduating from these programs enter the workforce at a higher level, and may have more options starting out as a result.

Where to find accredited programs

In 2007, the NVTA listed 140 accredited programs, with 16 offering a four-year degree; seven programs were described as long distance. Alaska, Arkansas, District of Columbia, Hawaii, Montana and Rhode Island are states that do not have such programs. Bel-Rea Institute of Animal Technology is well-known as the location for the popular show *Emergency Vets*.

Increasingly, accredited long distance learning programs, such as those offered through the AAHA (American Animal Hospital Association) or

Penn Foster College, allow candidates to obtain their veterinary technology degree when there is no program available locally. These long distance degrees also allow a person to attend school while continuing to work. If this is your route, you must have an approved credentialed technician at a local animal hospital sponsor you for your externship training. These distance programs are usually two years; just make sure the program you select is accredited by the American Veterinary Medical Association (AVMA). A complete list of accredited programs is listed on their web site, or you can just contact them for more information.

Exams

After graduating from an AVMA accredited veterinary technology program, students are eligible to sit for the NVTE, which is regulated by the American Association of Veterinary State Boards (AAVSB). The NVTE is offered twice a year, and licensing or certification is required by some states. The test is multiple choice, with 200 questions addressing all aspects of a veterinary technician's role including pharmacology, laboratory testing, farm and companion animals, record keeping, diagnostic and medical procedures.

Depending on the state you live in, technicians may be called licensed, certified or registered (LVT, CVT or RVT) with the general term "credentialed technician" applied to all three titles. The AAVSB is currently working to adopt more common standards nationwide; some states still do not have specific laws regulating the role of veterinary technicians in practice, so there are people who may work as "vet techs" but do not have the true education, experience or certification the title suggests. Many states have a practice act that defines what a certified technician can and can't do on the job. Although all states regulate the veterinary technology certification differently, they all require individuals to pass the NVTE. Additionally, some states require technicians to pass a state exam before becoming licensed. Most states allow the transfer of NVTE scores from state to state as long as the testing between the states is comparable.

Further Certification

After passing the NVTE, technicians may pursue specialty interests in areas such as emergency and critical care, anesthesiology, and dentistry. Gaining further certification in these areas requires the applicant to work as a credentialed technician for a minimum of three years in the field specified. There is then a year-long application process requiring recommendations, case study logs, skill set lists and evidence of a required number of hours working in that specialty over a three-year period as well as a minimum number of hours of continuing education in that specialty. If the applicant is accepted to sit for the exam, he or she is given a year to study for a multiple-choice, 400-question exam. Upon passing the exam, he or she can add the title "Veterinary Technician Specialist" (VTS) to his or her name.

Research technicians

Laboratory and research technicians must obtain a Bachelor degree to work in their field.

Those wishing to work in research need to gain certification from the American Association for Laboratory Animal Science (AALAS). Sitting for the exam requires having certain educational and hands on experience in a laboratory setting. There is a series of levels of these exams and testing is based on animal husbandry, facility management, animal health and animal welfare.

Continuing education

Most graduates of veterinary technician programs and credentialed technicians have years of experience in their field before passing the NVTE; many began working in a clinic during high school and continue during college. Veterinary technicians are expected to continue their education throughout their careers, including their day to day on the job experience. There are many opportunities to learn including trade magazines like Veterinary Technician, local and national conferences and on-line courses offered by groups like the Veterinary Information Network (VIN).

Zookeeping and Wildlife Management

Zookeepers and wildlife management career tracks require a minimum of a bachelor's degree in animal science, biology or some similar degree. In addition to schooling, hands-on experience in the field is usually needed. Specific experience with a particular species could help if the job you are looking for is in the same area of interest. Other experience can include jobs at veterinary clinics, preferable one that also treats exotic pets, local rehabilitation centers, petting zoos, ranches and laboratory experience. Competition for these jobs is fierce, and higher levels of education and experience tends to augment career options in this area. As with biologists and careers in research, education levels in the zoology field often extend to a Master's or Ph.D. The University of Florida and Michigan State have notable programs and are a good place to start your research,

Zookeeping

A zookeeping career typically requires a bachelor's degree in biology, animal sciences or some similar degree. Experience with the animals in a similar setting to the job you are seeking is also preferred, though this experience can include previous volunteer work. Some zoos may require their zookeepers to pass an exam before being hired. There are also health and endurance requirements for many of these jobs since they are so physically demanding.

Zoo curators

Zoo curators must obtain a master's or doctoral degree to gain employment. If you're interested in this path down the road, courses in zoology and anatomy are recommended as are English and writing classes, because you'll be writing articles or filling out grants. Practical hands-on experience in this area is required and may include volunteer positions, internships or work as a zoo keeper.

Zoologists

Zoologists, who conduct their own research or work in related administrative positions, normally have a Master's degree or Ph.D.

Breeding and Handling

Jobs in breeding, handling and training require a firm grasp of animal health, genetics, behavior and nutrition. A degree in animal science or some type of business schooling can help when running your own breeding business. Becoming a handler or trainer usually requires hands-on education and knowledge gained from being in the field and working your way up, but any education in animal behavior, animal science or business helps in getting started.

It's all about experience

Breeding animals, which can lead to handling and training or vice versa, is increasingly popular. Education for any of these types of jobs is usually hands-on, maybe even starting with your own pet. You will need to be knowledgeable about heredity, diseases and medical problems that may occur, proper feeding and housing of the animal you are breeding or training. Also, you'll need a business sense. Developing relationships with other breeders and veterinarians can be one of the most important ways to learn about this field. If you run a farm, you will most likely be breeding your own animals.

In this field, it's common that many who enter already have hands-on experience, whether from growing up with parents who bred animals, having worked closely with an owner or breeder of show animals or from working as assistants or technicians in animal hospitals and calling upon that medical background.

Dog trainers

Dog trainers have been in the spotlight of late, in part because of books and shows like *The Dog Whisperer*. If you're interested specifically in dog training, training programs exist across the country, so investigate options in your local area. You'll get a certificate for passing the course. An animal science degree with courses in animal behavior can also help here; this degree is required for research or zoo positions.

Working hands-on with a trainer and handling many animals helps to get started in dog training. Some veterinarians specialize in behavior and working for them will give you the experience needed to start a career. Forming good relationships with successful people in the field is crucial to maintaining a career in this area.

Horse breeding

In the horse business, there is more work available for handlers; look in trade magazines, ask around within the industry and visit local racetracks and breeding farms. But among your competition will be other workers who may have a lifetime of experience within the field and are known within the industry.

Other entry level training experience can come from circus or similar work, or for animal agencies that rent out trainers and animals for commercials, advertising photo shoots or films and TV.

Farming and Ranching

Most people who work on farms or ranches obtain knowledge of the animals and mechanical equipment via plain old hands-on experience. Though that kind of experience has always been emphasized in this area, schooling is becoming a more important part of staying competitive in the farming and ranching fields, even to people who were raised on farms. Education options include a two- or four-year college program in animal sciences, agriculture or ranch management. When starting your own farm with no family farming connections, the easy part may be the business half, whereas the animal husbandry and mechanical inclinations must be learned. College animal science programs teach farm animal husbandry and medicine and can lead to a career in farm animal or ranching. Some farms offer internships to gain this type of experience. Many associations are available to help small specialty farmers in starting up a new business.

Getting that degree

All state colleges provide degrees in agriculture through land grants. For example, Rutgers, Cook College Campus in New Jersey fulfills its land grant status through teaching and outreach programs within the agricultural and public communities. Their services include continuing education and certificate programs, work with youth groups, nutrition research and information and invasive species research and identification.

Farm managers with bachelor's degrees can go on and obtain master's degrees or become voluntarily certified as an Accredited Farm Manager (AFM) by the American Society of Farm Managers and Rural Appraisers after taking classes and passing examinations.

To find a job working for someone at a farm may mean looking for a fairly large-sized operation. You should be well-versed in current farming operation techniques, business trends and have knowledge of the animals you are working with. The bad news is that on a small farming scale, these jobs are almost nonexistent unless you are prepared to run your own farm. There are jobs to be found in the corporate farming world, but as stated earlier, this is not recommended.

Horse farms

Jobs on horse farms are easier to come by. Employees are always needed to help clean stalls and carry feed, and if you have experiences with horses, letting them out or riding them. Other farm-type jobs exist in places like petting zoos, facilities that offer pony rides or a local hobby farms.

Farm hands

Farm hands need not have any experience or specific education. They basically do the manual labor and are usually overseen by a higher-level laborer or manager. Farm hands usually receive on-the-job training and duties may be seasonal. There is high turnover, so work may be easy to find, but the pay is usually minimum wage and involves long hours.

Shelters and Animal Control

Workers in shelter and animal control jobs require at minimum a high school degree or GED. Becoming an animal control officer usually requires little more than a high school diploma and some animal experience to get started, though some states require courses in cruelty investigation, such as North Carolina. The National Animal Control Association offers training courses around the country, but most training is done on the job within the specific facility.

Animal rescue

Rescue work through an organization requires hands-on experience with animals. Many people start their own rescue programs and build relationships with local shelters to facilitate the adoption of animals they take in. The Humane Society of the United States, the American Humane Association and the National Animal Control Association offer training programs and workshops that can be helpful to people looking to enter this type of work. Topics include how to capture stray animals, guidelines for humane euthanasia, wildlife issues and how to work with the public.

Support staff skill set

More advanced positions in a shelter facility may require a college degree or specialized training related to the specific job. Animal control officers working out of a shelter may be required to have a "euthanasia technician" or "chemical capture" certification. Animal cruelty investigators require training in certain areas of the law whereas management positions require business experience or further degrees. Training and experience in supervision and management can be helpful as well. Some shelters need people to do their promotions, such as holding fund raising events, and a shelter may hire planners to oversee this aspect of the business.

Biology/Research

Researching and teaching

Although jobs may be found in biology or research with bachelor's degree, a Ph.D. is usually required for positions involving independent research or to move into administrative work. (Some jobs will actually pay for their employees to obtain a Ph.D.) A bachelor's degree will allow you to work as an assistant in a laboratory, testing or inspection job or to work in other areas related to biological science, such as working as a sales representative. If you take further courses in education, you may become an elementary or high school biology teacher. A master's degree is needed to work in applied science or product research or may be used to get in the door in terms of basic research. Candidates with a master's degree or higher also have the option of teaching.

An undergraduate biology degree includes classes focused on the sciences such as chemistry, biology and physics. Math and computer science courses are also required, because of the increased dependence on computers and computer equipment in a laboratory setting. English or some similar writing course may be helpful in you career when drafting testing proposals, writing for journals, applying for grants or in writing up test results. Courses in specific areas of interest are usually reserved for post graduate education, although electives in areas of environmental studies, marine science, microbiology or botany may be helpful. Larger colleges may have specialized departments in certain areas of interest, offering more opportunities for students whose interests are more specifically defined.

Further education, such as a master's program, is usually focused on a specific area of career interest.

Preparation for Other Professions

Practice, practice, practice

Jobs in categories like grooming, handling or kennel work usually start from a person's desire to work with animals and are simply learned through hands-on experience. Vocational schools teach courses in animal grooming and numerous resources are available to help in starting a pet sitting or dog walking business. Although it is not always necessary to have prior training, some form of experience in handling animals can help in landing a job in these areas. Pet sitting and dog walking may require more experience if you are dealing with pets that require medication. Some of these jobs can start in high school, but a GED is required to obtain any further formal education.

Working in or owning a kennel requires no special schooling; however, you should be familiar with the basics of animal care, potential diseases and know how to recognize and handle a situation needing medical attention. The same goes for pet sitting and dog walking. If you are putting yourself in a position where you will be caring for animals, you need to educate yourself, either through books or some other hands-on-experience, about how to work around animals.

Pet stores

Pet stores usually hire entry-level people and only sell "pocket pets" such as fish, hamsters and parakeets along with pet supplies. Because you will be selling products to consumers, you should possess a basic knowledge of animal feeding requirements and habits. If the pet store sells animals that you will be tending, you must know housing and feeding requirements and recognize any signs of illness. Larger pet stores require supervisors and managers, and these positions may require some type of business training.

More recently, pet stores have begun selling more exotic pocket pets that require specialized housing and feeding; these stores may require their workers to learn how to care for these animals. Employees may need to advise customers on a certain diet, cage set up or toys for their pet. Pet stores that sell puppies want workers who can recognize and act on illnesses the puppies may develop while under the store's care. These employees may also have a more active role in screening potential homes for these animals and would need to work with new pet owners in purchasing supplies and food and instruct them on how to care for the puppy once home.

Grooming

Grooming can be learned in high school work-study programs or through technical schools offering programs. There are state-licensed grooming schools available for 6 to 10 week sessions or for several months. Schooling can be a mix of classroom hours (some of which may be completed online) and hands-on training. Classes address subjects such as canine physiology, as well as how to cut and bathe. The National Dog Groomers Association of America offers a master grooming certification; this program trains an individual to groom for show quality and the exam consists of both a written and practical section. Trade shows offer seminars, whereas magazines such as *Groomer to Groomer* give business advice. After finishing a program, education can be furthered through working in a store or pet shop, or for a veterinarian or breeder.

Veterinary assistant

In the past, becoming a veterinary assistant required no special degree and many people have worked their way up to this position through entry level positions. Today, there are many online and long distance education veterinary assistant programs to get someone started in becoming an assistant.

Getting Your Foot in the Door

CHAPTER 6

Volunteering

There are many ways to get started in the animal field. Businesses tend not to hire entry level workers unless they have had some kind of training or hands-on experience with animals, but depending on what you're interested in doing, one of the easiest ways to get your foot in the door is to offer your services free of charge. Places like animal shelters and wildlife rehabilitation centers do not have money to spend on paid staff and they often look to volunteers to help get the work done. Some smaller veterinary clinics may take volunteers or entry-level paid workers with no experience whom they are willing to train from the ground up. Volunteers are typically limited in the amount of work they are allowed to do depending on the specific workplace and liability involved. Cage cleaning, feeding, administering basic medications as directed by a doctor and socializing non-threatening animals are a few of the tasks that volunteers do. Even organizing fund raisers or doing paperwork are ways to help out a particular association. The goal of such a volunteer experience is to see if you can handle being in the environment of the particular job you are seeking, as well as to get some entry level experience on your resume.

Learning about yourself

If you're looking to change careers into the animal field, a volunteer job can be a good barometer of your interest and fit, without having to commit. Volunteer hours can also be more flexible, so you may be able to commit to hours that don't conflict with a current job. You should be honest with the organization you are volunteering for and let them know you are interested in a career with animals, but want to see what it is about first-hand and make sure you are making the right decision.

Volunteers wanted at an animal shelter that needs you

Local animal shelters may be the most promising sources of volunteer work, as they consistently use volunteers. Positions are usually non-paying and involve minimal training and responsibilities, but can lead to other opportunities. Some volunteers also help with animal rescue and assist in raising orphaned domestic animals until they are able to be adopted out. Shelters also consult with or hire trainers, groomers, veterinarians or veterinary technicians to care for sick animals at the shelter. Working side by side with these professionals can give you a valuable training opportunity.

Most of these opportunities are easy to get as there is a high turnover rate and many positions are usually available. If you do not have a contact, just walk in to the facility in person and ask to speak to the person in charge of volunteers.

Where to Look: Entry Level

Newspapers and other sources

The first place to look for jobs is in the newspaper. This will give you an idea of what is available locally. In some animal industries, trade magazines can be helpful in locating a job. Veterinarians, zoos, medical research and farming industries all have their own journals and job listings are advertised in them. In these areas, an online search can be helpful.

All you have to do is ask

Not all places of business advertise for job openings on a consistent basis. Veterinary hospitals, for example, often have job positions open for entry-level or other support staff but don't advertise them—a quick telephone call to the human resources department or office manager may give you information about an open position. College campus research labs may advertise on campus, and groomers may just post "help wanted" signs on their front window. Pet stores usually advertise employment, especially the larger chains. If there's a specific place of business that you want to work in, by all means approach them.

Word of mouth is always useful in looking for a job. Ask friends and neighbors who have pets if they know of any facilities looking for employees. Let people know what you are looking for, even if they are not necessarily involved with animals. The connections people have can be surprising. If the jobs posted in the newspaper don't fit what you are looking for, it can still be beneficial to contact these employers to let them know what you are interested in. Someone may be able to point you in the direction of the job you want. Otherwise, there is a variety of resources to look to during your job search. At the end of this book, the appendix lists helpful web sites and addresses.

One job leads to another

If a job listing interests you but you don't feel you qualify, it still may be worth the effort of interviewing. Employers that advertise for a higher-level employee may be willing to take someone with lesser experience if they don't find another desirable candidate. Some positions may have been open for a long period of time and the employer may be willing to train someone just to fill the space. If you inquire about a position and are told you do not meet its requirements, ask if there are other openings that would fit your skills and education. Getting into an animal hospital as a receptionist could lead to a position elsewhere in the hospital. Once you take an entry level position, keep your eye on other positions open within the hospital and other job listings elsewhere.

Networking

Even if you do not get hired, ask the employer if it will keep you in mind for a future position that opens. Networking through any available opportunity is the key, and this shows an employer that you are still eager to work for it. Keep in mind that you may get information from the interview alone that will push you further along in eventually getting the job you want. If you have the skills and education required for the jobs you are applying for, but continue to interview and do not land a job, you may need to do some self-evaluation to see if something about your personality, approach or even a previous job reference is holding you up. If you are seriously up for the challenge, you might even ask an interviewer if he would honestly evaluate where you are lacking and go from there.

Internships

If you have a new veterinary degree and are looking for an internship, there is a national matching program that gathers information from both applicants and internship programs and then matches the veterinarian to the job they will take. Externships must be applied for and applicants are admitted based on interview processes.

Breaking in at a Higher Level

A more specific, non-entry-level position will likely involve more research—and a commute. It goes without saying that the more education and training you have and the higher-level job you are seeking, the more competitive the stakes—you may be considering a position that won't be within easy commuting distance or offer the best salary, depending on the competition to secure these jobs in the first place. Obviously, if you live in the city and are looking for a job on a ranch, expect to do a lot of driving or be prepared to relocate. If the position you're applying for is temporary (as with an internship) then a short-term relocation may not be as disruptive to your life. In some instances, four-day work weeks are becoming more common, with four longer days but a shorter week. This is typical of night and weekend positions and helps in keeping employees long-term.

Qualifying

Jobs involving higher degrees of education are not as flexible in terms of hiring those with lesser qualifications. There are state laws that must be followed in retaining a veterinarian to practice in a hospital. Some states require that a veterinary technician be licensed to practice certain medical treatments. Positions open to master's degree and PhD applicants will not be available to a person holding a bachelor's of science in agriculture. When applying for a position, know what's required versus what's recommended.

Where to look

If you have a veterinary technician degree or above, keep in mind that local private hospitals may not always advertise for job openings—a phone call may be necessary to get you an interview (this is also true if you are targeting a specific area of the country or a specific facility). Several trade magazines and veterinary journals (information can be found in the appendix) have advertisements for jobs throughout the country, and the larger private or university hospitals, pharmaceutical companies, research labs or shelters typically advertise here. In addition, there are online resources that post jobs specifically for the veterinary field. Veterinary societies may have job postings or message boards on their web sites, and large conferences usually have job posting boards available for anyone to advertise on. If there is a specialty you are interested in, do some research to find that specific clinic, or consult a journal targeting that area, whether it be emergency and critical care, zoo medicine or scientific research.

Many small clinics that advertise in the local paper have high turnover rates because of fewer career growth opportunities. But these hospitals can be a potential source of growth for an enterprising candidate ready to use his education and experience to help expand the business.

Selling yourself

Be sure to market yourself appropriately when interviewing for positions in the veterinary technology field. Hospitals can use your credentials to further their business as people want to know they are bringing their pets to professionals at the top of the field. Some technicians offer their services per diem and may work for relief services. They may then be called in to area hospitals who are temporarily short-staffed and that are in need of experienced workers.

Take advantage of this close-knit profession. Word of mouth can give you an invaluable lead on a job as many veterinarians keep contact with other professionals in their field.

Starting Your Own Business

People who have been working with animals for years may decide the next career move for them is to be out on their own. If you don't have experience working with animals, you may want to get a job or volunteer in the same or similar field to gain insight and make sure you are moving in the right direction. Either way, before starting your own business, you should first be sure you have what it takes to get the job done.

Your local college may offer free business services and counseling to people wanting to be out on their own and may even offer legal services at a discounted price. There are also over 300 organizations in the United States that offer microloans to start or expand a current business. These smaller loans can offer up to $15,000 and the companies offering them use less stringent standards for obtaining a loan than a traditional bank does.

Farming

When starting up a farm, you should consult with a financial advisor to see if your plan is viable. Be prepared with initial startup costs, including purchasing of animals, land, fencing, feed and veterinary care and then what yearly costs might be. You should be able to research your estimated income each year by consulting with associations related to the type of farming you will be doing. There are tax benefits associated with owning a farm, and reviewing the IRS *Farmers Tax guide* is recommended. Tax deductions may be included in land taxes as well as cost of feed, veterinary needs, travel related to business, maintenance and repair to any business related equipment and tax, legal, education and advertising services.

A place of business serving animals requires certain permits and regulations must be followed according to the town or city you are working in. In some states, support staff may own an animal hospital as long as they have a licensed veterinarian on staff, whereas in other states only veterinarians may own such a business. Opening a kennel often requires a certain amount of property that must be located a specified minimum distance from residents or water sources.

Pet sitting

A pet sitter may start with one or two dog-walking jobs on the side for friends and as word gets around, a pet sitting business is launched. Before starting your own pet sitting business, it is a good idea to work for an established sitter. (Look in the phone book or local paper for pet sitter ads.) Often, these businesses have positions open, but do not advertise them.

If you decide to start your own pet sitting business, you should research tax requirements, insurance and what other similar businesses are charging. There are pet sitting groups that offer advice to those interested in starting a business. Create an angle to attract customers and print up business cards to pass out at every opportunity. Associating yourself with a local veterinarian or pet store is a good way to attract business. Ads in local papers and in local stores may also bring customers. Keep track of where you're gaining most of your clients and refocus your advertising in that area.

Kennel

If you are looking to open your own kennel, you should first work in one and make sure it is the right business for you. You'll have to research the need for a kennel in the area, and familiarize yourself with the local laws (see above). Most areas have strict requirements as to where a kennel can set up business, and you may be restricted as to types and numbers of animals you can keep, the hours you are able to be open, and so forth. You may have an easier time opening a doggie day care than a full service kennel.

Pet store

When opening your own pet store, you will need to determine if you will be selling pet supplies only or if you will be selling animals, which requires greater expertise, staff and possibly licenses depending on the animals you're selling. You should be associated with a local veterinarian who offers emergency hours in case an animal becomes sick.

Being organized, informed and prepared are necessary in running any business. Records must be kept and you might have to supervise employees. Many veterinary conferences offer business-based lectures to doctors to help them in running their own hospital. Hiring or partnering up with someone who has animal-based skills and knowledge can also help. You should also thoroughly research the need for the type of business you want to start in your area and be aware of what your initial startup costs will be as well as the availability of commercial space to rent or buy. The prices you charge should be comparable to other similar services in the area and by offering coupons or specials in the beginning you may attract a clientele more quickly than relying on advertising alone. But be careful of offering the lowest price as it gives the perception that your services will be of lesser quality than of a business who charges slightly more for the same service. Be prepared to spend most of your time with your business and realize you will have little time off. A business related to animals can be a rewarding and profitable venture, but as with any business, you will need to work hard and be prepared to keep up with trends to keep customers coming back.

Do your homework

These days, most organizations' web sites offer insight into the company philosophy and list names of people that work there, hours of business, location and more. You should be well-versed as to a given company's information; and company web sites may help you answer specific questions for that particular job. You should then make a phone call to the organization to make sure the information you have is up to date and get the name of the person who is in charge of hiring and ask to speak to him or her. This is the person to whom you will address your resume cover letter. Don't rely only on information gained from the web site since it may be outdated.

Face time

If you are able, it is a good idea to visit the business to drop off your resume in person. Not only will this guarantee that it arrives there, but you will also be able to see the physical environment and get an idea of the type of work environment and employees that already work there. If you are able, try to ask a few questions of the people working there before leaving and let them know you are really looking forward to interviewing. Many times, this first impression can be a way in the door.

If you are able to speak to someone in charge of hiring on the phone or in person before applying for the job, be prepared to market yourself for the position on the spot. If you do not have the specific requirements listed for the job, let the person hiring know you are willing to train and do what it takes to gain those abilities. For entry-level positions in particular, many employers would rather hire the right personality than someone who solely has the right requirements. The ability to be flexible with regard to the hours you can work, tasks you will take on and salary you can accept could put you ahead of other applicants. A follow up call a week later to check the status of the job opening could bring you new information and another shot at the job.

The Perfect Resume

Include as much relevant information to the job you are applying for on your resume, but keep your font consistent and format neat and legible. In some cases, a creative format or inclusion of an item of personal information about yourself can make your resume stand out from the others; use your judgment when it comes to the kind of job you're applying for. You can vary between bold, underlining and font size, or use a unique letterhead or paper color to catch a prospective employer's eye, but make the resume as a whole look uniform. It is most important to remember to keep your resume professional, tasteful, uncluttered and to the point.

The basics

First things first: your name, address and phone numbers where you can be reached. List your schooling next, or if that is less relevant to the job you are applying for, your experience and skills. You want to target your resume to a specific employer and job, emphasizing the aspect of your experience or skills that show you can do whatever specific job you're applying for. In describing your skills, use technical terms. If you are new to the field and unsure of the exact wording, keep it simple.

You should also list any relevant papers you have written for journals, clubs you participated in, pets you own or hobbies you have. Last, list three references that relate to the field to which you are applying. If you do not have three related references, the references should at least show a professional relationship to you. Employers do not want to see personal contacts. Ask your references' permission to list them, and get their current contact information. Include their professional title, business they work for and telephone number.

Entry level vs. higher level

If you applying for an entry level position, it's best to keep your resume to one page, highlighting any animal experience you have, no matter how small. For higher level jobs, list all relevant education and degrees gained as well as all pertinent information to that position. Higher-level resumes can be two to three pages long and follow the career of the applicant up to that point. Below are two sample resumes to help you get started.

Entry-Level Resume

Jane Smith
111 smith road, smithtown, nj 11111
Phone (555) 555-1111 * Fax (555) 555-111 * E-Mail smith@smith.com

Objective: At this point in my life I am looking to begin a long time career working with animals and I believe that a job as a veterinary assistant is the ideal start in achieving this goal.

Experience

June 2005 to present, *The Kennel,* New York, NY
All aspects of pet care.
My responsibility is to answer phones and make appointments, take in boarders for overnight or day visits, give any medications as needed, bathe, walk and socialize boarders.

May 2003 to June 2005, *Barker's Grooming,* Smithington, NJ
My job consisted of making appointments, communicating client's wishes to groomer, taking payments
I eventually trained as an entry level groomer and assisted with brush outs, nail clipping, ear cleanings and baths.

Education

Sept. 2002 to present, *Smithtown Community College*, NJ
Associates in Biology in progress

Sept. 1998 to May 2002, *Smithtown High School*, Smithtown, NJ
Graduated. Focus of classes was in the sciences. Member of Animal Science Club
Honor Roll for four years.

Other Interests

Breeding canaries, volunteer work at the local shelter, reading and hiking.

References
Mary Smith (555) 555-111, trainer at Barker's Grooming
Barney Smith (555) 555-1111, owner The Kennel

Experienced Resume

Curriculum Vitae
Jane Smith
111 smith road, smithtown, nj 11111
Phone (555) 555-1111 * Fax (555) 555-111 * E-Mail smith@smith.com

Education
North Carolina State University—College of Veterinary Medicine
Residency in Emergency and Critical Care
Raleigh, NC July 2004-present
VECCS Candidate; General Examination: passed in May 2005

The Medical Center for Pets
Small animal and surgical rotating internship
New York, NY June 2002-July 2004

Cornell University—College of Veterinary Medicine
Doctor of Veterinary Medicine
Ithaca, NY June 1998-May 2002

Rutgers the State University
Bachelor of Science
New Brunswick, NJ June 1994-May 1998
Major: Animal Science

Research Experience
North Carolina State University College of Veterinary Medicine
Research advisor: John Smithson, DVM, Ph.D., diplomat VECCS
September 2003-November 2005, Researched correlation between full moon and seizures in animals.

Rutgers the State University – Department of Physiological Sciences
Research advisor: Bob Smithson, Ph.D.
May 1995-May 1996, Studied the effect of high fat dog cookies on Beagle stomach lining.

Publications
Smith, Jane. Increased Trauma in Dogs During Summer Holidays. J Am Vet Med Assoc. 2001 Mar 05;332-338.

Smith, Jane. Behavior of Clients in Emergency Situations. Abstract ACVIM 2005 Annual forum. JVIM 2005; 40(5): 630-675

Professional Presentations
Abstract presentation, 22nd Annual VECCS Forum; New Orleans, LA; September, 1999: "Emergency response to beagle in distress."
Emergency Medicine Rounds, The Animal Medical Center; New York NY; April 2003: "Utilizing catnip to arouse an obtunded patient."

Related Experiences
Volunteer Work: Bergen County Zoo, Paramus, NJ
July 2003, Assisted staff veterinarian in emergency procedures at zoo and was on-call
Externship: Good Dog Clinic, Smithtown, NY

June 2001, Rotation through triage and emergency services
Externship: Catnip for Cats, Smithtown, NY
October 2001, Rotation through spay and neuter surgery clinic
Student Technician: Rutgers the State University, New Brunswick, NJ
September 1996-May 1997, Instruction of underclass students on laboratory procedure, handling of laboratory animals, venipuncture and care of laboratory animals.
Tutor: Rutgers the State University
September 1996- May 1997, Tutoring of groups of students in basic level biology courses

Awards Received
The Golden Stethoscope Award- to the final year student excelling in veterinary studies; Cornell University, May 2002

The Charles Darwin Prize- for excellence in the study of Beagles; Rutgers University, May 1998

Academic Achievement Recognition, The Smithtown Student Organization, May 1995

Enrollment Incentive Scholarship, 1994-1998

Summa cum Laude Award, May 1993

Professional Associations
American College of Veterinary Emergency and Critical Care – candidate, 2000-present
American Veterinary Medical Association, 1998-present
American Animal Hospital Association, May 2002-present
Student Chapter of the Veterinary Emergency and Critical Care Society, 2003-present
Pre-Veterinary Club, Rutgers University, 1994-1998

Extracurricular Activities
Hiking, reading, travel
Language
Fluent French
Knowledge of Spanish

References
Carlos Smith, DVM, Diplomat VECCS
Emergency and Critical Care Department, North Carolina State University
Teaching Hospital 11111 Smith Rd, Smith NC 11111. Tel: (555) 555-1111

O. S. Smith, Ph.D.,
Rutgers University Department of Laboratory Sciences
1111 Smith Rd., Smith NJ 11111. Tel: (555)555-1111

Pete T. Smith, VMD, Ph.D.
Catnip for Cats
1111 Smith Rd., Smithtown NJ 11111. Tel: (555)555-1111

Cover Letters

You will need to create a cover letter to go along with your resume. This should convey to an employer what specific skills you have and how you can contribute to the organization in question. The cover letter is also where you can show some of your personality and give a sense of your work ethic and goals. If you know something about the specific business you are applying to that shows why you want to work there, this is the place to mention it. But keep the cover letter short. Do not mention specific work hours or salary requirements (unless directed to do so).

Sample Cover Letter

March 9, 2008

To Whom It May Concern,

Your advertised job posting looking for a veterinary kennel worker in "The Local News" caught my attention. I was drawn to the ad by my strong interest in both animals and the medical field.

Although I do not have experience working in this kind of environment, I have extensive animal experience with my own pets, currently two Great Danes and a teacup Yorkshire terrier. I have also been trusted to watch pets while my neighbors have been away.

My current job as an office assistant is no longer fulfilling and I wish to work in a job that I find more rewarding. I am interested in becoming a veterinary technician, but would like to gain firsthand experience in a well-respected workplace like yours. My schedule is flexible and I'm confident that my ability to learn quickly along with my love of animals will make me a good match for this position.

I would like very much to discuss this opportunity with someone from your business. Please feel free to contact me at your earliest convenience.

Thank you for your time and consideration.

Sincerely yours,
Jane Smith
111 Smith Rd.
Smithtown NY 11111
(555) 555-1111
smith@smith.com

The Interview

CHAPTER 8

Getting Ready

Once you have an interview scheduled, you have some more preparation to do. Whatever position you are applying for, before the interview, review any information you have about the company to which you are applying. Know the general departments or services they offer, what the details of your job may be and what the hours are. Come up with some specific questions about the organization or specific job you're doing beforehand to demonstrate your interest in their business.

What to bring

Bring along extra copies of your resume, and if there is an application to fill out, obtain it before the interview and fill it out beforehand. Make sure you write neatly and fill in all the blanks—even if the information is on your resume, that doesn't mean you can skip it on the application. Be tactful when filling out information that asks about why you left your previous jobs. Reasons such as "looking for better opportunity" or "looking for more benefits" are acceptable, whereas "nobody trained me" or "pay too low" are not. Keep your papers in a neat folder or briefcase.

Be aware that many employers are now beginning to search prospective employees through Google or similar internet search engines. The internet is a public forum and information may be legally found there, even if it may not be accurate. If you have accounts with chat sites such as MySpace.com, make sure you are representing yourself appropriately in case a prospective employer comes upon it.

First impressions

The importance of dressing appropriately for an interview cannot be stressed more. You are trying to make an impression; conservative attire is the best choice. Particularly in animal-related fields, people often show up to interviews for entry level or volunteer jobs in inappropriate attire. Dressing professionally will put you ahead of the pack. At the same time, be sensible. Be prepared to get a tour of the facilities by wearing comfortable but professional-looking shoes. High heels are not going to make a good impression if you are being shown around animal exhibits in a zoo.

You should show up at your interview 10 or 15 minutes early. This will give you a chance to relax before the interview, and you may also be able to observe some of how the office operates. Keep in mind that your interview starts the minute you walk in the door, and the person hiring may ask other employees their impression of you. You relay a lot of information about yourself through body language and tone of voice. Give the impression that you are interested, respectful and prepared. Compliment the business in some way. If you are nervous and you are worried this is showing, bring it up to the interviewer in a positive way. A simple statement such as "I'm very nervous right now because I really want to work here and I'm excited about this opportunity" can help to relieve the stress you are feeling and will put any possible negative impressions in a different light.

At the Interview

There's no typical interview for an entry-level position. An interview can last half an hour to an hour, and you may or may not be given a tour of the facility. For higher level positions, interviews will take more time, lasting anywhere from one hour to half a day. You may be asked back for a working interview so that a prospective employer can evaluate your knowledge and skills and to see how you fit in with the group.

During an interview, be careful to keep your responses informative, but to the point. An employer does not have time to sit through long stories about how you raised a litter of piglets when you were 10 years old. He or she wants to find out if you have the education, skills, experience and personality to fit the position, and will ask follow up questions if he or she needs to. Make positive statements out of possibly negative ones. Being honest is the best way to answer interview questions, but make sure you do not criticize past employers or workers. Speak about your skills honestly and express interest in learning new tasks while letting the interviewer know you are highly trainable.

The following is a list of sample types of questions that are typically asked in an interview. For the most part, there's no right answer to a question; interviewers are more interested in the way you answer particular questions. Are you tactful and professional? Are you familiar with certain aspects the job requires and are you willing to be trained further if needed? Do you show a desire to work in the specific field?

Questions to expect: entry level

• How did you hear about us?

Employees like to hear good things about their business. If you know of someone who recommended their facility or had a favorable experience there, mention it here, with any details. You are applying to a reputable establishment; mention how you want to work for the best.

• Why did you apply for this job?

Almost all applicants respond with "I love animals." This is a good start, but be more specific about any past experience in working with animals or future goals within the industry. Do not go into detail about nondocumented past experience such as an animal you rescued, but do mention that you found the experience rewarding.

• What were some of your responsibilities at your last/current job?

Be specific here, even if you only did entry-level work. Show that you have a working knowledge of what you did learn and that you're ready to build on that experience. For example, if you cleaned cages, demonstrate that you know why this is important by saying "I was responsible for keeping the animals clean. My daily rountine included proper cleaning of all housed animals, which was an important part of keeping infections down within the facility." Refrain from using terminology that is not familiar to you. It will not impress the interviewer if he or she thinks you are using words you do not understand.

• What skills do you have for this job?

Talk about your skills in a straightforward way and avoid embellishment. Let the interviewer know you are eager to learn more.

• Why did you leave a particular job?

It is best to be honest here, yet do not give away any information that is not asked. The usual response to this question is along the lines of, "I want to learn more and experience a better working environment." Keep the focus on the future, not past employment. If you think a situation at a previous job will come up when an employer checks references, you should discreetly mention it here (without putting down any former employers). If you were fired from a job, show that you understand why and have learned from it; emphasize that you are willing to admit mistakes and learn from them. At the entry level, employers may be more willing to take a risk on someone, especially if the candidate can show he is ready for responsibility.

• Describe a difficult situation at work and how you handled it.

Keep this answer humble. A good reply would be to describe a simple, common work-related incident and how you used proper channels to address it. Show that you are a team player as well as being a problem-solver.

• Are you willing to work overtime, holidays, weekend hours?

You will need to be as flexible as the job demands. But do not say "yes" to working hours you know you cannot commit to, even if it costs you the job. Instead of flat out saying that you can't work specific hours, see if there are other arrangements that can be worked out. For example, if an employer is looking for Saturday hours and you can't do a full day, offer tor work a half day or every other Saturday. Entry level positions are where most people pay their dues, filling in the shifts more senior staff do not want. However, if you want the off hours because it fits your schedule better, use this as a reason why you should be hired.

• What are your salary and schedule requirements?

If the employer does not mention salary and schedule, you should. This is a big part of the decision, and it is best to negotiate when you are sitting face to face. Entry level jobs in the animal industry area not high-paying. You should have a salary range in mind that you're comfortable with, and you should be aware of when raises and evaluations are done within the company. If you have specific scheduling requirements, bring them up now. If you are flexible, be ready with the amount of hours a week you are able to work. Let the employer know if you are available to work last minute if someone calls in sick or if you will have more work availability during school breaks.

• Do you have any hobbies?

Mention a few things you do outside of work and keep them to a list of things you do currently. You can talk about your pets, but try to mention at least one thing not animal-related. Listing too many interests may be a warning sign to an employer that you overextend yourself and lack focus.

Midlevel: (degree required [AA, BS] for position) questions

• How did you get into this field?

Be ready to discuss any previous courses or jobs you have had that have prepared you for this one.

• What relevant coursework do you have?

Sometimes just mentioning a degree is sufficient, but it's helpful to be prepared to discuss a few relevant courses you took.

• What experience do you have?

Although education is a requirement for these jobs, outside experience may be what actually gets you in the door. Mention any related jobs or class projects that underscore your experience level. Mentoring from a specific teacher could be mentioned here. You might talk about how an experience in your past speaks to the job you're applying for, or how you may have been researching the position.

• What are some responsibilities you've held at other similar positions?

Talk about your role at any previous job or within a class (research project or lab partner). You can even talk about your role in a job-related club or volunteer experience. Focus on what you gained from your position and how you developed to the point you're at now.

• What are your short-/long-term goals?

Short-term goals usually refer to the next six to 12 months, whereas long-term may imply five years or so. Have a list of three to five goals for each. You can include a personal goal, especially if it is linked to your job—for example, telling an employer you'd like to buy a house five years down the road shows him you're motivated to work towards a pragmatic goal. Midlevel jobs tend to be more steady than entry-level positions, so talking about a future role you can play within the establishment is something the employer wants to hear. It wants to see employees grow with a company.

• Will you be looking to further your education?

Some jobs require employees to continue education during their employment, and may even offer compensation towards this end. If you honestly don't know the answer to this question, you can ask what type of education an employer recommends as your next step. If you are planning on furthering your education, an employer will want to be certain that any classes don't conflict with your potential work schedule. If educational pursuits require that your work schedule be altered, it's important to assure an employer that you would remain with the business during and afterwards.

Professional level (veterinary or master's degree required) questions

• Why did you apply for this position?

Professionals on this level are looking for a work environment that fits their professional and personal style. Some positions may only offer short-term employment whereas other openings may have the potential for lifelong employment. At this level, there are often yearly contracts at which point the position is re-negotiated.

• How do you feel about working off-hours/long hours?

Increasingly, veterinarians or those in higher education jobs are not willing to consider working weekend and off-hours. (Many feel like they have put their time in doing internships or working at previous jobs.) But unless specifically stated, you can expect to have to work some off-hours and to stay late at times, because working with animals is never predictable. However, you certainly do not have to be on call 24 hours a day. If you're concerned, ask if there's more specific information on what long hours/after-hours entails, and have an honest conversation about what you are able and willing to do. There may also be options to change schedules down the road. If you are able to shadow or spend some time in the facility before taking the position, you can discreetly ask other employees about this.

• What case/study in particular did you find challenging?

Have a specific example ready here. Without going into minutia, you should describe a case that shows how you identified a problem, researched possible solutions in a timely manner, communicated the information and arrived at a positive result.

• Why do you feel you are a good fit for this position?

Just stating that you are good at your job is not enough. Get that point across, but also emphasize other ways in which you will also be an asset to the business—whether contributing to staff development, helping to create a team atmosphere or any other tangible skill you feel you can bring to the table.

- **What would you do in situation X (particular to the job you are applying for)?**

This is where you'll need to show advanced problem-solving skills and flexibility. You may need to ask questions about policies within the facility, or know medical information or state laws that will help in your decision making. The employer wants to hear a decisive answer that shows you are knowledgeable about your field.

- **What do you feel you can offer to this business?**

Here you can mention a relevant example from past experience. If this is a job where you will have clients and your past record shows you have a faithful following, this would be good information to emphasize..

- **Who do you admire within the profession?**

The person you mention is less important than the reason you give for why you admire them. Talk about some values that attract you to this person. These values should reflect your own.

- **What are your short/long-term goals?**

Again, have a list of three to five goals for each. (See midlevel interview questions, above.)

Other Considerations

For higher level positions, you may interview with a group of interviewers. They will be weighing your personality, previous experience and your grades to rate you against other applicants. Your knowledge will be tested, whether you're asked what you might do medically or ethically in a specific situation. Unlike most of the questions above, these questions usually do have a right and wrong response based on current medical information, laws in effect and the employer's philosophy.

Awkward questions and negotiations

Be aware that there are certain questions you cannot be asked during an interview, such as your age, marital status, religious beliefs or number of dependents you have. If you are asked questions like this, tactfully decline by replying "I'd rather not answer that question if you don't mind."

If the salary offered is not as high as you expected, be honest, but tactful. Ask what benefits are included or if overtime pay is offered. You can ask when you would reasonably expect a raise or promotion. These questions show an employer that you are willing to work within given constraints, but be sure to remind the interviewer of your skills or education if they are a match for the position. You might suggest that you are willing to work off-hours for a higher salary. If your current salary is higher and your current job is similar to the one you are applying for, you can say that you would like to match your current rate. Don't give a definite yes or no answer at this time based on salary or hours that are not to your liking. Many times, if an employer wants to hire you, it may be willing to negotiate later on. (This is not true of internships and government jobs, which usually do not offer any flexibility as to salaries.) Keeping yourself open to all possibilities can make or break a dream job.

Asking questions

The interview is not only a time for your employer to quiz you, but an opportunity for you to ask pertinent questions regarding a job you may be doing. It is just as important for you to find out if the job and organization is a compatible fit for you. Any questions you ask should be specific and relate directly to the job you will be doing.

After the Interview

Be prepared in case you are immediately offered a position. (Although this is not often the case, it does happen, although most employers will want to check your references before offering a position.)

Following up

Before leaving, find out when you can expect to hear from them. If the time by which you were to be contacted passes, a follow-up phone call is in order. If you leave a message, briefly remind the employer who you are, ask if a decision has been made and request that someone contact you at his or her convenience. (Be sure to leave your phone number.) If you still do not hear anything, you may want to consider if you want to work for a place of business that does not return your call or contact you within the timeframe given. Keep any correspondence courteous and thank an employer when it does respond. If you don't get the job, the interview process is still good practice for the next opportunity.

After your interview, you should immediately write a follow up thank you note to the person who interviewed you. Mention (briefly) one or two things you like or feel you can contribute to the company.

Passing the test

Many of these jobs now require drug tests before an actual job is offered. This is usually done through an independent lab and the business offering the job will pay for the test. The results may take two to three days.

Making the transition

If the job meets all of your requirements and you're willing to take it, let the employer know how much notice you'll need to give a current employer and when you can start. If you are asked to do a follow up or working interview, have your planner with you so that you can schedule this.

Alternatively, if the job is not what you expected or if you have some reservation, be honest and see if something can be worked out. Either way, thank the interviewer(s) for his or her time, especially if the employer is one you might want to apply to in another capacity in the future. For this reason, if you are later called and are given the position, but have accepted another job, return the call to let them know your status.

CAREERS

ON THE JOB

VETERINARY AND ANIMAL CAREERS

Lifestyle Issues

CHAPTER 9

In the following chapters, we'll discuss further the career track for veterinarians and other animal professionals. But first, we'll talk about basic lifestyle issues and salary to expect.

The Basics

Be flexible

In general, working with animals demands flexibility with scheduling and pay. This can be especially true at the entry level. If you are first starting out in a field, schedule flexibility may in fact be the reason you got the job! Animals require care around the clock—night, weekend and holiday hours need to be staffed. There are jobs where you may need to be on-call in case of emergencies or if other staff is out sick. Some days don't go as planned, and you may be required to stay after hours. Breaks are usually taken when and if opportunities arise and lunch can often go missed on busy days.

Mental and physical demands

Physically, jobs involving animals can be demanding. Many times, employers may be understaffed and the rest of the workers are counted on to pick up any slack, no matter what your position. There can be heavy lifting involved, hours of being on your feet, cleaning up all kinds of bodily fluids, multiple job hazards including working with chemicals and handling the animals themselves, and multitasking heavy workloads. For example, working on a farm involves long days that start before the sun comes up and may not end until long after sundown. There are no days off, seasonal weather extremes, heavy food barrels, cumbersome equipment and the handling of large animals.

Along with demanding hours and physical labor, there are emotional highs and lows to deal with, and high stress levels can cause a career to burn out quickly if not managed properly. Seeing sick or suffering animals on a daily basis can be depressing if not balanced by the positive feeling that you are providing a valuable need in helping the animals you are working with. Dealing with difficult clients can be a source of constant stress. In certain high-stress environments, lack of teamwork can cause employee conflict.

Continuing education

Jobs with animals almost always require constant continuing education to keep up with the latest information, no matter what the field. There is rarely time at work to keep up with this information, so you'll have to do this on your own time, whether through a combination of continuing degrees, internet research, online courses or mail-in long distance courses, subscribing to professional journals, attending conferences or joining groups/organizations of other like-minded professionals.

Salary

The pay scale can be underwhelming. Many animal professionals start their careers with such a strong urge to work with animals that salary is almost secondary to job satisfaction. But entry level jobs that pay low salaries may have other benefits including medical, on-the-job training and a yearly allowance to pay for outside training. For higher-paying jobs, a correlating level of education and/or licensing is expected. But generally, careers with animals aren't at the top of the pay scale, and those who pursue higher levels of education often wind up having to pay off student loans for years after they have graduated. One thing to keep in mind is that the animal field is constantly experiencing an increase in employment choices and needs, and with that, salaries will follow suit.

Career Changers

In this industry, career changers aren't unusual. Whether someone finds their current work unfulfilling or just wants out of an office job, a number of people in this industry move into this line of work to satisfy an emotional urge of helping animals. On the other hand, you may already work with animals in one aspect, but wish to explore a different field of animal work.

Before quitting any established job, it is a good idea to research the options. Visit various jobs and observe the daily expectations. This is where jobs with night, weekend and holiday hours are convenient. If extra schooling is necessary, before signing up for classes, it may be wise to find an entry level job to test out the chosen path. In this industry, there are many jobs that can be "tested" with part-time work before making the jump.

Career Snapshots

CHAPTER 10

Every job is different, and careers taking care of and supporting pets can vary widely. In this chapter, we'll discuss the nuts and bolts of different careers, including information on salary, day-to-day responsibilities, career paths, uppers and downers.

First Stop: Veterinarian

Once you graduate from veterinary college, you must pass an exam to become licensed within your state. Many graduates are now entering into year-long internships with teaching facilities to gain a wider range of experience in a short amount of time. These internships can then lead to residency programs, usually lasting three years, to become a specialist. These days, vets are no longer expected to be jacks-of-all-trades.

The AVMA recognizes a list of 20 specialty boards including Cardiology, Orothopedics, Behavior, Nutrition, Emergency and Critical Care, Microbiology and Zoology, Some of the more traditional routes of veterinary practice are in general practice, surgery, internal medicine, emergency and critical care and government jobs in agriculture or research. Other jobs can be found in veterinary pathology, laboratory, behavior, animal shelters, teaching or lecturing, zoos, aquariums, wildlife rehabilitation or on farms.

Salary and benefits

Pay depends on specialty, level of experience and geographical area, but it is also important to note that because of the school loans most veterinary students have accumulated during their college years, it can be difficult to get ahead monetarily until they become established in the field. Most veterinary jobs start in the area of $50,000, working up to $129,000 or more for experienced specialists. Entry level (right out of veterinary college) and internship or externship programs offer low wages, typically in the range of $26,000 per year. Jobs in government, animal shelters or on a local college faculty are some of the lower paying veterinarian jobs, starting in the $30,000 range, but they offer more structured schedules and benefits. Work in private research or in laboratories usually starts at about $50,000 while also offering a more traditional schedule. Established vets can lecture at conferences, where they'll receive pay for their services based on lecture hours and are usually paid a predetermined amount for preparation time, travel, rooms and some meals.

If you have your own practice, your salary will be determined by how many hours you work and how much you charge for your services balanced with how much you spend for equipment or traveling time. Another factor here is what benefits you will offer to your employees.

Most jobs in the veterinary field, especially government, university or in large hospitals, offer benefits including medical benefits, paid time off, uniform allowance, continuing education allowance and retirement plans. Some clinics may take on partners as part-owners of the business.

Uppers

Veterinarians have the ability to save lives and educate clients and staff. The job offers tons of options—there are many specialties and different types of job locations. If you want to relocate across the country, you can! And when you finally do land a steady job, your salary will reflect the number of years you put into your education. As you establish yourself in the profession, you'll be able to dictate your work hours and build a following of regular clients. With a support staff among whom you can delegate tasks, you will be free to make proper diagnoses and to talk with clients. Finally, there is always something new to learn and the job is never boring.

Downers

But veterinary college is long and, as previously mentioned, very expensive. If you go into an internship right out of college and you have loans, you will not be making enough money to pay them off right away. In addition, competition for internships and externships is fierce, and you may have to relocate to get one; you may also need to relocate if you decide to specialize.

Sometimes, veterinarians feel they're not playing as much of a hands-on role with the animals, given all of the office work—from dealing with clients to writing estimates, making phone calls and documenting information in a patient's record. These duties can sometimes distract from the main work, which is coming up with the best medical plan for a patient's constantly changing medical status. Some patients may be difficult, and veterinarians need to ensure the safety of their staff. In addition, there are always difficult clients, some of whom may not pay their bills.

An Inside Look: Veterinarian

Meg Julian, VMD, Emergency and Critical Care Veterinarian

Meg works evenings and weekends at a large emergency and referral animal hospital. She assesses patients who present for emergency visits, reassesses hospitalized patients, and forms treatment plans in collaboration with patients' owners. She also educates owners and educates and assists interns as they treat their patients.

How did you get into this field?

I have always enjoyed spending time with animals. In school, I discovered an aptitude for math and science and interest in medicine, so I decided to pursue a career in veterinary medicine. My yearlong veterinary internship after veterinary school exposed me to emergency and critical care.

What are your hours?

I rotate evenings and weekends, usually starting at 4 p.m. and leaving between 12 a.m. and 3 a.m.

What is a typical day for you?

4:00 p.m.: I'd arrive at work and round with the day doctors about cases they have been treating in the hospital.

5:00 p.m.: I provide written updates about these hospitalized patients to the telephone receptionists so that they can update owners as they call. I then review cases with interns and do serial reassessments of in-hospital patients.

5:00 p.m.-11:00 p.m.: I triage and assess incoming emergencies and for any cases I take on, I review the patients, order diagnostics (like blood work and radiographs) and review the results and then discuss a plan with the owners. If the pet is admitted to the hospital, I write up admit and treatment orders. On some nights I may need to do minor surgery or procedures such as laceration repairs or place urethral catheters in patients with urinary obstructions. I may need to tap the chest of patients with heart or lung problems. On a good night, I may get the rare opportunity to take a break to eat or go to the bathroom.

11 p.m.-12 a.m.: Before I leave, I round with the overnight doctors about cases that are in the hospital. On a slow night, I might leave at midnight, but usually it winds up being much later.

What do you like most about your job?

It's difficult to say because I like really almost everything about my job, including working with people, striving to provide the best care for animals and helping owners to make the best decisions they can within their means.

What do you like least about your job?

Dealing with cases where we cannot find the cause of illness.

Do you have plans to further your career?

I plan to keep on attending continuing education classes so I can continue to practice the best medicine possible.

How has your career/field changed over time?

There are more advanced diagnostics available, such as ultrasound, digital x-ray and MRI, and we are able to get blood test results back more quickly. People seem to value their pets and the relationship they have with them more. There is also more specialization within the field, such as critical care, dentistry, radiography, oncology and rehabilitation.

Do you have any advice for someone entering the same/similar career?

Make sure you like medicine, not just animals. You must be compassionate, but emotionally stoic enough to maintain composure in sad situations so that you will still be able to advise distraught owners. Schooling is long and expensive and the salary for most veterinarians is good, but not anywhere near what practitioners for people make.

Animal Health Care Technician (Veterinary Technician)

Credentialed veterinary technicians can branch out into a number of different specialties, either medical or in management, as discussed previously. They might also teach a veterinary technology course at a college or lecture locally or nationally at conferences. There are jobs within private or university research labs, shelters and in zoos. Once you gain your basic certification as a technician, your experience will dictate where you go within the field.

Salary and benefits

Salary for veterinary technicians is usually based on experience and education the individual has, as well as the kind of facility and the area of the country. Because there is no current regulation in the field, figures vary from practice to practice and state to state. But across the board, salaries have steadily increased of late because of the higher public demand for veterinary services and the increasing value placed on pets—people are more willing to pay for more expensive medical care, and this is reflected in technicians' salaries.

Private practice offers some of the more diverse salary ranges, sometimes starting at $10/hour up to $20/hour. More advanced certification or management experience can bring in higher salaries in the $60,000 per year range. If you are inclined to work weekend, holiday or overnight shifts, you may earn more money from pay differentials that may be offered. In particularly busy clinics, time and a half may be paid for working overtime. Benefits again depend on the clinic, but more hospitals are now offering paid time off, uniform allowance, health insurance and retirement plans in an effort to stay competitive. University hospitals and corporate laboratories usually offer benefits typically found in the business sector.

Uppers

Burnout in the veterinary technician field is not as prevalent as it used to be, because of the continuing diversity of the field, expanding job opportunities and increase in pay (all of these developments are directly related to the more current national requirements that technicians pass the NVTE). As animals will always need medical treatment and places of refuge, these jobs will continue to be available, in an array of different roles. And if the veterinary technician role is right for you, you'll find that there is always more to learn, and an unlimited amount of available resources to draw from. And at the end of each day (literally and figuratively) you'll know that you've made a difference in an animal's life.

Downers

On the downside, although the veterinary technician role is gaining more credibility because the more stringent educational requirements needed to find work, not all jobs treat technicians according to their abilities. At the same time, in certain instances, support staff for vet techs still lack necessary experience, making risk of injury greater and increasing the workload.

Another issue is that although pay has increased, it's still difficult to live solely on a technician's salary, which often does not meet cost of living.

An Inside Look: Veterinary Technician

Doreena Schiavi, RVT, Emergency and Critical Care (ECC) Night Supervisor

Doreena is a credentialed emergency and critical care (ECC) veterinary technician and a night shift supervisor at a specialty hospital in Bergen County, NJ. Her duties include triage and nursing for critical animals—placing IV catheters, performing phlebotomy, taking x-rays, intubating and resuscitating animals when they stop breathing and much more. As a supervisor, she writes and implements protocols for the rest of the staff to follow. She attends supervisor meetings to resolve staff issues and to brainstorm new ideas, and is also responsible for dealing with any issues arising during her shift.

How did you get into this field?

I was always fascinated with animals, bringing home every stray you can imagine. When I was in high school (16 years old) there was an announcement over the school PA system that a local vet hospital was looking for help and I thought, "that's the perfect job!" When I first started, my job primarily entailed a lot of cleaning and caring for the animals. I've worked in this field ever since.

What are your hours?

I work overnights, primarily on the weekend, from 8 p.m. to 8 a.m.

What is a typical day for you?

8 p.m.: As soon as I get into my CCU ward I immediately check all my patients' treatment sheets and make sure they have the appropriate IV fluids, they are on appropriate medications and no treatments have been overlooked. I check any discrepancies with the ECC doctor.

8:15 p.m.-8 a.m.: I get a rundown of all of my patients from the technical staff that I am relieving. Throughout the night, I have treatments that have to be done on an hourly basis, from basic flushing of catheters to more complex responsibilities like obtaining a central venous pressure on an unstable patient. Between these treatments we also have emergencies that come in throughout the night, so I may be busy placing IV catheters, drawing blood, taking x-rays, assisting the doctor in laceration repairs, or preparing an animal that will undergo emergency surgery.

8 a.m.: At the end of my shift I fill out nursing notes and give a written and verbal rundown on all of my patients to the technicians coming in for the day.

What do you like most about your job?

When I have a comatose animal come in, and with the proper medical attention, it recovers and you put your face down to give it a kiss and the animal licks you right back. There's no better feeling in the world.

What do you like least about your job?

When an animal has to be euthanized because the owner does not have the money to treat the pet and they are suffering from a life threatening ailment.

Do you have any plans to further your career?

The ultimate plan would be to go back to school and get my degree in veterinary medicine, but for the time being I am going to concentrate in becoming an ECC specialty technician.

How has your career and field changed over time?

I have been in this field for over 20 years and the degree of overall care has greatly changed and improved. Dogs and cats can have MRIs done on a routine basis and owners are more apt to go to great lengths to save their pets. Animals are treated more like a family member than a piece of property.

Do you have any advice for someone entering the same/similar career?

A lot of people think that working with animals is full of puppies and kittens and nothing but play time at work, but jobs in the veterinary medicine field encompass more than that! You have to be dedicated to your job and your patients. There is a lot of cleaning involved, from accidents on the floor and in cages to animals soiling themselves, and you have to give baths often. You also need a strong stomach. We see many things that would make a weak stomach very queasy, from broken dangling legs to maggot infested rabbits. The last think is you have to be emotionally strong. Unfortunately you do deal with a lot of death. You get attached to a patient and feel their loss just as badly as their owners do. If you think you can handle all of these scenarios, then the veterinary medical field is definitely a career you should consider.

Pet Service Industries

Entry-level positions such as pet sitting, dog walking, kennel, grooming and pet store work are often taken on as supplements to another part- or full-time job.

Salary and benefits

Employment opportunities are fairly easy to find, but earnings in these careers can be low. If you start your own pet sitting, dog walking or grooming business, your salary will obviously depend on how much business you take in and what you charge will be based on your client's needs. You should set up a payment scale related to services you will provide and time spent on each job. These charges should be adjusted yearly as needed. You will need to declare taxes to obtain future loans or collect social security. You should keep track of mileage put on your car, gas used and any other expenses incurred related to your business. Meeting with a financial consultant is recommended. Membership in a pet sitting group may help in finding information related to the industry. If you work for a pet sitting business, you may already have your taxes taken out and you may be offered benefits such as gas reimbursement, uniforms and health insurance. If you wind up expanding and hiring other employees, you should get involved in a local business group to help answer questions related to keeping staff.

Pay for working in a kennel or as a groomer also varies as to the part of the country you're working in and type of services offered, but usually start from minimum wage and up. Groomers may get paid commission based on the number of animals they work on, and tips may be included. Benefits may or may not be included depending on the business. As with dog walking, if you run your own business, you will have to keep track of your overhead expenses, such as advertising and supplies. You may need to rent out space or equip a van for door-to-door grooming services.

Pet stores also usually pay from minimum wage and up, depending on your experience and position, with managers making more. Most of the larger chains offer benefits such as vacation time, store discounts and health insurance.

Uppers

You can use this kind of job as a stepping stone toward a higher goal in your career. Irregular hours may fit around a school schedule or other activities. There is constant hands-on contact with the animals, something that can get lost in other positions, such as in higher education. Also, in these fields, positions are always available because of the high turnover rate.

Downers

But jobs in these areas can be physically and emotionally exhausting. Heavy lifting, bending, noise and handling of difficult animals is the norm. Animals may need to be euthanized because they are old or unwanted, and you most likely will come across animals that were abused. The work, not always mentally stimulating, quickly becomes repetitive. Days are long and salaries may be low, and your hours may be irregular or fall on weekends, nights and holidays. On the job training may not be offered or available. Moreover, the high turnover rate means there is a steady stream of workers coming in as replacements, and your job may not be secure if you are not willing to put up with some of the negatives.

Inside Look: Pet Store Manager

Mike Dolan, Store Manager, PetSmart

Mike is in charge of overall running of the store, including hiring/firing employees, making employee schedules and overseeing employees' training schedule. In addition, he trains all new store managers for other stores. He orders supplies, deals with day to day situations that arise, and ensures that animals are being cared for properly.

How did you get into this field?

I worked in other retail stores before being hired by PetSmart as a store manager.

What are your hours?

6:30 a.m.-5 p.m., six days a week.

What is a typical day for you?

When I get to work I go through my e-mails and plan my day from there. I go over scheduling of employees and resolve any scheduling conflicts. I walk through the store to make sure everything is neat and clean for when the store opens. When shipments come in, I help unload them and review and approve the order. As the day progresses, I walk around to see how everything is going.

What do you like most about your job?

I enjoy interacting with the public. I also like animals (I have two cats, one that I adopted from the store) and enjoy educating people about basic animal care. I'm able to offer them products that make owning a pet easier.

Do you have plans to further your career?

I would like to eventually get into human resources.

How has your career changed over time?

Pet stores used to be mom-and-pop operations, with one person or a family owning and running the business. Now pet stores have turned into large corporations and they need managers to run each separate division.

Do you have any advice for someone entering the same/similar career?

In retail work, be prepared to work long hours. Take opportunities to train further as a supervisor or manager and continue to seek out further opportunities as they arise.

Day in the Life: Pet Sitter

6:00 a.m.: Drive five miles down the road to walk Spike, a Shar-pei who never lets you into the house immediately. This is your last day of a five-day pet-sitting job; Spike's "parents" went to Aruba for vacation and you've been visiting him three times a day. Spike has no medical problems, but his temperament makes him one of the more difficult pets you have to watch. As you approach the house, you hear him barking inside the door. You are glad that you put the gate up in the entryway to give you some distance and time to calm him before approaching. You enter the house and Spike looks as ferocious as ever, but you have his favorite treat ready. Eventually you are able to step inside the gate, put the leash on him and take him for a walk. You feed him, clean his bowls, straighten up, and leave a final note, which is Spike's report card for how he did while his owners were away. You then leave the envelope with the bill for your services and a return envelope. The entire visit took 1 ½ hours.

7:30 a.m.: Return home, eat breakfast, shower and get ready for your next client.

9:00 a.m.: Appointment with new clients. They have four cats, two of whom have medical conditions (one a diabetic and one with early stage renal failure). Your local veterinarian recommended you because he knows you have the experience to give the attention the cats require. The clients live about 15 minutes away and will require you to come help give treatments and take care of the cats on some weekends they're away. You find the house, meet the cats and go over the medications needed for each cat, along with feeding instructions and emergency numbers. You go over your qualifications, reiterate the schedule they have left you, and answer any questions they have. You will be starting over the weekend, and as with all new clients, you ask for an initial deposit for the first job. Once they are regulars, you will leave a bill after each job. This initial visit took one hour and 15 minutes.

12:00 p.m.: A lunchtime walk for Rosie, the beagle you visit three times a week. She is a longtime client, and at 10 years old, is spunky and loves to go to the park to play. The walk is 30 minutes, with 15 minutes spent in the park, for a total of 45 minutes. Rosie's parents leave the $20 for the visit on the counter for you.

Day in the Life: Pet Sitter cont.

1:30 p.m.: The day has been going more smoothly than usual and you have some time to run your own errands. Today you are having new business cards made and will post some advertisements in the local groomers' and pet stores.

4:00 p.m.:: To supplement your pet sitting, you work part-time at the local pet store cleaning the cages (they only sell "pocket pets" such as hamsters, gerbils, guinea pigs and rabbits) and making sure everyone is fed and healthy. You work a four-hour shift until 8.

9:00 p.m.: Do some research online and review your upcoming schedule before bedtime. You are looking into taking an online course about pet first aid. Next week is Labor Day weekend and your schedule is full, with six different pet sitting clients, which is the most you will take on at one time. The rest of the week looks pretty slow, which will give you time to prepare for the busy weekend coming up.

Breeding, Handling, and Training

Except in a controlled setting such as a laboratory, jobs within the breeding and training category are not well defined, at least in terms of what's understood as career progression. Many people start on their own and gain experience in different ways. Some breeders are well-known, or become well-known, within their circles. There are certifications for training that can enhance your reputation while you try to establish yourself.

In breeding, handling and training, an important aspect of building a respectable career is seeking out well-respected and knowledgeable people who are already established in the field. They are sources of valuable advice and can also provide other connections in the industry. You may even discover a breeder who might need extra help around the kennel. (Typically, established breeders don't require extra help and are probably not willing to pay for it.) This kind of networking means that travel is often necessary. But be respectful of breeders' time.

Salary

Breeding salaries vary considerably depending on where you live, the type of animal you are breeding and how much breeding you do. According to the Department of Labor, the median yearly salary for breeding jobs is $26,820. If you have an animal science degree and breed for the farm, horse or research industries, you can potentially make considerably more money, sometimes charging per animal bred. Horse trainers may also double as breeders and may charge up to $1,000 per month to work with a horse; as such, if you gain a reputation for breeding good stock, your work will increase. If you are in private business, typical base salary is approximately $31,000; a government job pays similarly but may offer better benefits and job security.

When it comes to salary, keep in mind that as a breeder, your first and foremost reason for getting into this type of career is to care for the animals you breed, find good homes for them, and to hopefully contribute to the breed in some way by furthering a superior genetic trait. The money made is secondary—hopefully, with some good business sense, your initial investment will multiply and allow you to continue your breeding program. There are too many unwanted animals in the world and unless your goal is to breed the best of the species you choose, you should not get into this field.

Horse handlers are some of the higher paid in the field as are dog handlers for top breeders. Working for research breeding facilities pays starting at $15.00/hour whereas zoo breeding programs are usually handled by the overseeing veterinarian and is included in his or her salary, which is often government funded.

The pet side

Starting a breeding program takes time and money. Be prepared to put down an initial investment before you begin to see some return financially. You'll need to purchase a breeding female and a stud or stud services (or you can opt to start a stud service only). Pregnant animals have greater nutritional needs and require frequent visits to the veterinarian to mark their progress.

When it is time for the female to give birth, you must prepare a proper area for her to nest down. For horses, you may need to pay someone to stay up and watch for the foal to be born or set up cameras that will alert you to the birth. If the mother is having trouble giving birth, she may need surgery (C-section), which may occur during emergency hours. If the mother becomes ill while she is nursing, you may need to bottle feed the babies.

Once the litter matures, you'll need to oversee their feeding and vaccinations. Some breeders have dewclaws or tails docked by their veterinarian, whereas others choose to have ears cropped, which must then be maintained until completely healed. At this point in the process, there are countless hours spent cleaning, feeding and socializing the litter while looking for suitable homes for the offspring. With experience, you will decide which of the litter are "show quality" and which are "pet quality" and decide on pricing appropriately. Some breeders offer money back after the buyer shows proof of neutering their new pet.

The people side

You will hopefully gain experience on matching the right animal to the right home, but this involves screening potential homes and letting people visit with the animals and/or send photos. Many breeders maintain web sites with this information easily accessible to potential buyers. If you are selling to someone who lives far away, you may have to arrange for safe transportation of the young to their new home. You must also be prepared to take back any of the litter that are not working out for any reason. Sometimes breeders are left with some of the litter that do not sell and they have to decide on whether to keep them or adopt them out as they grow older. All of these expenses may play into your pricing of the animal. Other considerations are the size of the litter, the quality of the parents and the specificity of the breed. It is not unusual for pet stores to charge over $1,000 for a puppy from a "puppy mill" without proper papers; breeders are responding by charging $1,000 and up for their home-raised puppies with proper papers.

Breeding animals should be taken seriously and only when you are sure you have the time, money and are prepared to do what is best for the animals at all times. It is no longer acceptable to have a litter of puppies from the family dog just so the kids can see nature first hand.

Typical Timeline

Pre-breeding:

When the time comes to breed your first litter, make sure you are current on housing, medical and nutritional needs of the animal you are breeding. It is a good idea to consult with the veterinarian you will be using to set up a timeline for during and after the pregnancy. You should also prepare ahead of time any forms or ads you will need after the litter is born, since at that point you may be too busy helping to care for the young and the mother (while also caring for any other animals you may own). This is where your kennel club breeder contacts will come in handy. If you are breeding an animal registered with a particular association, they can usually help with the language and content of any contracts you develop for the sale of the litter. If you are working with another breeder and are using their animal as a stud for your female, you will need to determine who will house the couple while they are mating. You will also need to negotiate payment for these services. Some breeders allow first pick of litter for their stud fees, while others require monetary payment. You should make sure you're dealing with a reputable breeder, that the stud has proper registration papers and has been screened for any contagious diseases. It is not unreasonable to ask to see written certification from stud dogs you are using for the first time. If you do not, you may be exposing your kennel to unnecessary problems. You may also want to have a contract outlining the terms of the breeding in case the mother doesn't become pregnant the first time. The conditions should be clear for both parties. Again, clubs or other breeders can help you come up with wording for these contracts. Beware of anyone who scoffs at the idea of showing proper forms or who doesn't want to sign a contract. This should be a warning sign. A good breeder will recognize that you are not experienced and will help you along in the process.

Day 1 of pregnancy:

Once the mother is pregnant, you will need to seek out a veterinarian's services to make sure everything is going as planned.

Days 20-30:

Your veterinarian will examine the mother and may do an ultrasound screening to see how many young there are and monitor their development. They may have you change the mother's diet and tell you what signs to look for as the pregnancy evolves.

Day 61-63:

Once the mother is ready to give birth, you should have a quiet, comfortable place readily available. This is not the time to be inviting friends over for the big event. Make sure you're well-versed in recognizing signs of complications during the delivery, and have the number of a 24-hour emergency veterinarian available in case there are questions. There are some breeds that often encounter problems when delivering babies, and a C-section may need to be performed. This is a costly procedure, and post-surgery, a mother may not be able to nurse the puppies at all times. (This is also true with young first-time mothers, so you'll need to be prepared to do this for her. If you decided to breed a Rhodesian Ridgeback, there could be up to 14 puppies to care for!)

Assuming the birthing goes well, you will still need to monitor the mother's health as well as the puppies' growth. Eclampsia is a condition that mothers may get if they were not fed properly while pregnant; it causes a low calcium level, and symptoms include inability to produce milk, fever and shaking. This condition must be treated by a doctor and the puppies may need to be hand-raised after.

Puppies: Age 3 days:

Some breeds of dogs have ears cropped and tails docked; you should consult with your veterinarian for theses services. Even if you are not selling show-quality animals, you may want to reconsider having these procedures performed as many people now like the natural look of many of these breeds. Having dewclaws removed within the first few days of birth is recommended to avoid later complications; vets will also check for other health issues like cleft palate or heart conditions. If you did not screen the stud properly, and you have weak members of the litter, you may see problems like feline leukemia or other infectious diseases that are transmitted in cats.

Age 6 weeks:

The puppies will need a routine checkup and the first set of vaccines.

Age 6-8 weeks:

When the young are ready to be sold, all buyers will have to be screened thoroughly. Although recommendations for homes from people you trust are the best, breeders often have to advertise to find homes for the litter. Many breeders have certain standards for homes that they stick to. One time-saver is a short phone survey to screen out any homes that aren't a good fit. If the buyers seem promising, it's best to have them come see the puppies so you can evaluate them in person and see how they interact with the animals. Keep it informal, but you should have some questions ready for this meeting as well. If you get an uneasy feeling about a person, defer making a decision to sell to them.

Some prospective buyers may live out of your driving range, but may have recommendations from a breeder that you respect and trust. In these cases, you'll have to rely on a telephone interview and you should be prepared to send photos for them to see. If the sale is complete, you may need to arrange for transportation of the baby to its new home, either by ground or air. This involves meeting the requirements of the transportation company used and making sure the young are in top health condition to be transported. This can be a stressful event for a new animal, and if the plans are not thought out and coordinated properly beforehand, you could wind up with a sick orphan.

You should have a contract, signed by the buyer, that outlines specifics of what is required of them. You should also go over the details of the contract verbally. If you require the buyer to register the young with a club, you should have the documents and paperwork ready for them. You should also note in the contract that if for any reason the sale does not work out, the buyer must return the animal to you at no cost. This shows that you are responsible and that you care about the animals you are breeding.

Some breeders require that the young they sell are neutered or spayed at a certain age. They may offer money back from the purchase price upon proof of the neutering or spaying to ensure this is done. All medical costs, planned and unplanned, should be thought out carefully beforehand—limited funds should never compromise the animal's welfare.

Uppers

As a breeder, you'll be working from your own house, which has its benefits. At the same time, if you enjoy traveling, animal shows are a great excuse to see someplace new. Most breeders love what they do, and networking with people who love what they do can be rewarding in and of itself. No day will be boring!

Downers

But breeding can be quite expensive and deceptively time-consuming. For those reasons, a breeding career should be thought out carefully beforehand. Although breeding can be a good hobby for someone who is at home a lot, you must be prepared to make frequent visits to the veterinarian, spend many days and nights nursing sick or orphaned animals, recognize health defects in offspring, and screen new homes for the litters you raise. You must be prepared to pay for any unexpected medical expenses of the animals under your care, even if this means a loss to your end profits.

Farming and Ranching

There is no question that consumers have influenced the way agriculture is run today. A demand for more animal products at a cheaper price with a disregard to how these products are obtained has been the trend until recently, as worldwide production of these products caused an influx of foreign goods and precipitated the rise of the domestic corporate farm.

But as discussed earlier, the farming landscape is slowly shifting. The U.S. Department of Labor predicts that although overall work in traditional farming and ranching is on the decline, specialized small farming is on the rise. Many people are leaving their jobs in urban cities to return to nature by starting their own "retirement" farms, such as alpaca, bee farms or small goat or chicken farms, and selling their products locally. With current health scares like salmonella and hormones in animal products, consumers are becoming more aware of where their meat and dairy products come from. Many people are searching for safe alternatives and look to local produce for that security.

Career tracks

Many farming roles fall under the entry-level category, as previously discussed, and thus career tracks are limited. Below are some of the options in this field.

Manager

Historically, farm managers simply inherited the position as most of these businesses were kept in the family. Today, generally, a business degree (+/- a BS in animal science or equivalent) is standard for this position. As discussed earlier, farming involves long hours, and this is true of the manager as well, who is responsible for hiring, bookkeeping, networking, overseeing and training staff. Some of these duties may be seasonal.

Breeder/nutrition/husbandry

There are varied levels of experience within this category, and varied levels of education required, but lab workers, farm consultants and breeders all tend to have a minimum of a BS. Hours may be regular (laboratory setting or farm consultant) versus varied (horse farm worker/breeder) depending on the specific job. In these farming jobs, you'll need to make decisions about the lives of animals and know how to deal with different life stages of the species you are working with.

Sales/business owner

These more desk-oriented jobs tend to call for the highest levels of education, with a business degree (BS in animal science or equivalent) necessary, plus some further education in management. These jobs are usually quite time-consuming, though corporate jobs may have steadier hours than those of small business owners. In this kind of work, you'll get out of the business what you put into it, though there's less time out on the floor or in the field with the animals.

Salary and benefits

Today, most family farms rely on outside income to continue to exist. This may include renting out land for other uses, logging land that hasn't yet been cleared, renting out equipment or actually taking on a second job as supplemental income. Many family farms do not rely on government programs to keep running.

Salaries in the farming and ranching fields vary yearly depending on weather, price of farm equipment, and the profit the business takes. If you do not have experience working on a farm or ranch, a college degree could get you work on a higher pay scale than a farm hand would get, especially if you are hired to manage some aspect of the business. Larger farms and corporate factory farms hire at this level, as do agricultural colleges that have research farms on campus. Farm hands, ranchers, and other workers in these fields are usually in these jobs more for the lifestyle than for the pay—they'll tell you they gain satisfaction from working off the land without coworkers and bosses constantly looking over their shoulder. According to the Department of Labor, salaries may range from $17,000 a year for a farm or ranch hand to $31,000 a year for animal breeders. Benefits are not usually offered, but sometimes room and board and/or meals may be provided in lieu of full pay. But again, often the real pay is being outside, working off the land.

Uppers

Consumer demand for a better product that is treated humanely and without chemicals is changing the industry for the better. And small specialty farms or educational farms are growing increasingly popular. The organic farming trend looks like it will sustain the industry, but farming is never going away—one of the basic human needs is food and people will always need animal farmers as a resource.

The lifestyle can be addictive; working in farming means working outside with animals on a daily basis. Numerous resources include help from state college cooperative extentions, and more and more conferences held within the farming community with workshops on various topics from how to advertise your business in today's market to different farming techniques.

Downers

On the downside, small farms are still hard to come by, and the alternative is corporate farms, which are relying more on automated systems to raise and care for animals. And there are many variables in farming, from weather to uneven sales. The constant care animals require means that your vacation time may be limited or nonexistent. The job can be physically demanding, with heavy lifting and large, sometimes dangerous animals. If you're short-staffed or just a tiny operation, you may have to split your day into working hands-on with the animals and dealing with the business end of the farm—a combination that can be overwhelming for some.

An Inside Look: Alpaca Rancher

Richard Gyuro, Alpaca Rancher, Alpacas at Lone Ranch, Sams Valley

Richard feeds 50 alpacas morning and afternoon, and keeps the pastures clean. He administers shots (worming and immunization) twice a year, and supervises breeding of the ranch's females as well as visiting females. He occasionally assists with birthing, and is also the chief maintenance man, fixing whatever needs fixing.

How did you get into this field?

My wife, Renate, was an arts organization fundraiser and I was a sales manager for a national company. With our two daughters grown and gone, we were looking for a change from the corporate life in a large metropolitan area. Initially, we thought of semi-retirement, operating a retail business in a small coastal community, but we discovered alpacas and knew that we could still change the fundamentals in our lives.

We made the move away from the big city to acreage adjoining a rural community. Animals peacefully grazing the property were an important part of the vision of our new surroundings. An article in the paper about a woman raising alpacas caught my attention, and I began my research on the internet. Soon our weekends were occupied with visits to alpaca ranches throughout northern California and Oregon. A trip to visit my sister in Colorado was a good excuse to visit more alpaca ranches along the way. We also attended regional alpaca shows in Oregon. We were hooked, and in love with these gentle creatures

What are your hours?

While the work can easily be done by one, at Alpacas at Lone Ranch, we enjoy sharing the activities associated with alpaca ranching and easily find time to share in outside activities too. A typical day involves:

7:00 a.m.: Coffee, planning the day's activities while enjoying a view of our herd of 50-60 alpacas peacefully grazing.

8:00 a.m.: Morning restocking of the feeders with hay and feed supplements. Refill and refresh with clean water. This is the time when we calmly interact with each alpaca while carefully noting its state of well being. We have dogs, cats, and other pets to feed and visit too.

10:00 a.m.: Clean and sweep poop and dirt from the barn and paddock areas for neatness and to aid in parasite control.

11:00 a.m.: A trip to town for errands and stops at the post office, bank, and market. Time to meet friends for lunch.

1:00 p.m.: If a female is ready for breeding, the herd sire is escorted to her pasture. Alpacas breed for approximately 20 minutes, with the male emitting a continual guttural sound appropriately named "orgling." We begin halter-training young alpacas at about six months of age—20 minute sessions, two to three times a week for two weeks and an alpaca will go anywhere with you.

2:00 p.m.: Analyze and record information to maintain accurate animal and business records. Initiate and respond to communications with alpaca customers and the alpaca community.

3:00 p.m.: Plenty of time for non-ranching activities.

7:00 p.m.: A stroll through the pastures to check on everyone's well being before retiring for the evening.

Superimposed on the average day are occasional workdays filled with other activities:

- Herd health day: veterinary examinations, vaccinations, and toenail trimming.
- Hay and feed restocking: we have help in storing several tons of hay for the winter.
- Shearing: once each year, alpacas are shorn. There are a variety of avenues for adding value to your fleeces by having it processed into end products, such as yarn for knitting and weaving.
- Trade shows: two or three times per year we elect to attend two- to three-day events filled with education, show competition, alpaca auctions and sales. Transportation to and from can be easier than you might think.
- Customer visits: although many sales occur at shows, at auctions and over the Internet, many customers visit personally to view our ranch and our animals for sale. For those new to the industry, a free ranch tour is the best way to explore what alpaca ranching is all about.
- Birthing and newborn care: birthing days are frequently both the busiest and the most exciting days of the year.

Do you have any advice for someone entering the same/similar career?

We have been very successful as a medium-sized ranch, however, some others have not. Discussions with many newcomers indicate the following as important ingredients for fiscal success.

- Love of the animals, such that routine care is smoothly done by the owners without employees.
- Acknowledging the business aspect of alpaca ranching and following a simple marketing and sales plan.
- Being in a financial position to take full advantage of the many tax benefits.
- Luck—the birth of females facilitates sales and herd growth. While the odds are 50/50 for males and females, at times one or the other can seem to predominate and thus slow or speed the process.

Shelters and Animal Control

Reality television shows depicting animal control officers investigating calls has put this profession in the spotlight of late. Larger cities that have shelter programs offer the best opportunities for this type of work, and entry-level jobs helping in kennels can be easy to find because of high turnover from emotional burnout combined with low or no pay. Higher-level positions within shelter work include shelter manager, trainer, veterinarian or veterinary technician, animal control officers, and those who handle adoptions. As discussed, these roles require greater training and experience, and are also harder to come by since employees in these jobs tend to keep them for longer periods of time.

Salary and benefits

Like much of the other animal work discussed in this guide, most of the "pay" from shelter and animal control jobs comes from the pure satisfaction of helping animals directly or from educating the public to treat animals more humanely. Salaries start anywhere from minimum wage and up depending on the specific job, the training and experience you have, the program you are working in and geography. Private shelters may not offer the same benefits as a state governmentally run shelter, but may pay more. Higher training translates to higher salaries: managers and investigators can make $12,000 to $24,000 per year in a small community or $50,000 to $85,0000 in a larger city.

Uppers

Those who work in shelters and animal control know every day that they have impacted an animal's life. Rescue, animal welfare and pet adoption is hands-on work with the animals, but administrative and fund raising work can be just as rewarding. The opportunity to help educate the public about responsible pet ownership is also gratifying.

Downers

Shelter work is also mentally and, depending on the position, physically demanding. Not only are you exposed to difficult animals in difficult situations, but you need to be able to negotiate dealings with the public and possibly with government officials who dictate what will happen at your facility. Even among staff, diplomacy can be key, as shelters and animal control work finds employees and volunteers at an array of different experience levels trying to work together, and the stress of continual contact with potentially diseased animals can take a toll. You will most likely come across abused, sickly and old animals that have no chance of getting a home and who may even need to be euthanized. And budgets can be limited, especially considering the massive amounts of work to be done. For all of these reasons, the burnout rate is high.

An Inside Look: Animal Control Administrator

Bill Comery, ACO, ACI, Administrator of Animal Control, Borough of Paramus, NJ

Bill is the animal shelter manager for the town of Paramus, and is responsible for a staff of three to four ACOs. He establishes staff policy and procedures monitors their work daily. His job also requires him to interact with the AC veterinarian, the general public and other professionals and elected officials. He checks and monitors the shelter operations and may act as an ACO if needed, responding to emergency calls. Bill does initial animal cruelty investigations, and may work with the Bergen County Prosecutor's office on further investigations as an ACI. He is also responsible for establishing an operating budget and making sure expenses don't exceed the available funds. He also has to keep himself current on new regulations and procedures.

How did you get into this field?

This job was added to my current job responsibilities (as Director of Shade Tree & Parks Commission) by my employer. Since I've been in the position, I have obtained my Animal Control Officer (ACO) and Animal Cruelty Investigator (ACI) certification.

What are your hours?

Daily, Monday through Friday, 7 a.m.-4 p.m., and on call as needed. The animal control job is part-time in addition to my full-time Shade Tree & Parks position.

What is a typical day for you?

I oversee the staff, reviewing whatever work they do during the day and monitor the shelter, responding to any concerns that come up. From there, my day could involve anything—no two days are the same.

What do you like most about the job?

I enjoy being able to save an animal's life. We are a no-kill shelter. We actively rescue feral cats, rehabilitate them and adopt them out after proper medical care and socialization.

What do you like least about your job?

People who abuse and/or mistreat pets—there are people who think that pets are objects, not living creatures. Also, outdated regulations.

Do you have plans to further your career?

The governing body may expand our program to other municipalities with inter-local agreements in the future, which would expand my job responsibilities.

How has your career/field changed over time?

Financial constraints and budgets are tight, and we have learned to do more with less. New regulations from the state to improve animal care are always welcome, but sometimes require more funding and more work.

Do you have any advice for someone entering the same/similar career?

Many animal control officers suffer from burnout. You can't let your emotions overtake you—you must care, yet be practical and fair. The job can be as interesting and rewarding as you make it; the potential is unlimited.

Zoo, Exotic and Wildlife Management

Jobs in this field involve possibly frequent relocation or travel. Post entry-level, senior or head zookeeper positions are typically obtained by gaining experience on the job.

Salary and benefits

As always, salary depends on the education and experience the candidate holds. A government wildlife job hovers around $30,000, whereas a zoological park position can pay up to $80,000.

Uppers and downers

For professionals in this area, it can be thrilling to have the opportunity to learn about wild animals while caring for them in captivity. In zoos, many animals develop strong bonds with their caretakers, which can also be exciting. More zoos are developing and emphasizing natural environments for the animals in their care, and zoos increasingly serve as environmental advocates and sources of information for the public. If you're involved in zoo breeding programs, you may be helping reintroduce an endangered species to the wild.

But all of this excitement makes these jobs pretty difficult to come by. Competition is quite strong in this field. In addition, work can be demanding physically, and, moreover, dangerous as dealing with wild animals can be unpredictable. Flexibility is required, because hours can be variable depending on the animal needs. A good deal of travel may be required for research, and relocation is more common in these jobs.

Day in the Life: Zoo Caretaker

Below is a typical day in the life of a zoo caretaker.

7:00 a.m.: Check in on the animals, looking for any small changes and inspecting overall health.

8:00 a.m.: Prepare breakfast, which includes chopping fruits and vegetables, weighing hay and feed, adding vitamins and placing in appropriate dishes.

9:00 a.m.: Feed the animals

11:00 a.m.: Clean and disinfect the exhibits. Replace bedding as needed. This is the most time-consuming part of the job; it is important to make sure all the animals remain clean and comfortable. Some animals will need to be cleaned and groomed at this time also, although most animals groom themselves.

2:00 p.m.: Train and stimulate the animals. Some of the animals can be taught to take certain medical treatments without the aid of restraints. All animals need some type of activitiy to keep them mentally stimulated while in captivity. This may require some creativity on your part.

5:00 p.m.: Public presentation of one of the animals on display in the area you're working in.

6:00 p.m.: Last feeding and inspection of animals

Throughout the day: fitting in exams and medical procedures that arise, as well as any unexpected situations.

Biologist/Research

These jobs are found in the private and public sector; more than half of this work is governmental, including areas such as public health, national defense and agriculture. Pharmaceutical companies are another big employer here, as are hospitals, private labs or private research operations. As previously mentioned, companies like Pfizer and Abbott Labs have animal divisions, and act as resources to the veterinary community by offering in-house training and providing funding for many of the national conferences.

Career tracks

According to the U.S. Department of Labor, biotechnological research is driving job growth in this field. But there is growing competition for basic research jobs, as most employees now hold PhDs; in addition, the number of grant opportunities available for research projects is expected to slow down, increasing the competition for these grants. As these research jobs become more difficult to obtain, candidates are seeking jobs in the private sector.

Jobs in middle ground-arenas such as marketing, sales and teaching are more readily available. Some areas of biological science are mainstays of opportunity, like environmental regulation, botany and zoology, yet the number of opportunities tends to be limited because of the relatively small size of these fields. New company growth is slowing as businesses and laboratories merge.

Entry-level workers in this field typically find caretaker work in a kennel. This can be an effective way to gain access to a career with animals in a laboratory setting.

In a lab, technical assistants assist whoever's in charge of the particular research project. They may help with paperwork, conducting the experiment and caring for the animals.

Breeding of laboratory animals is another career track here, usually requiring at least a BS in biology or similar courses. Well-known suppliers tend to be are well regulated.

To work as a laboratory facility inspector also requires a BS or higher in biology or a similar degree. Successful candidates here have experience in the field, and travel is a part of this job, as inspectors need to travel to inspect various facilities.

Researchers and scientists have a PhD or some higher education (DVM/VMD/MD), and may be independent or employed by a business. Hours are usually regular, and a lot of time is spent in paperwork, looking for money and sponsors, collecting data and writing papers.

Managers oversee the whole of the laboratory. They do the hiring and firing, they make sure projects are going as planned and that funding is coming in. They are responsible for making sure the facility meets all standards.

Salary and benefits

According to the U.S. Department of Labor, median annual earnings of biochemists were $68,950 in May 2004. Entry level positions earned less than $33,000, whereas more experienced and educated employees could earn more than $100,000. Zoologists and wildlife biologists make an average of $50,000 depending on the specific job, as well as their experience and education.

Benefits vary. Government and private industry positions usually offer medical benefits, paid time off and retirement programs. Private researchers may need to fund their own health insurance depending on the agency they work for.

Uppers and downers

Research and academic jobs are usually among the higher-paying jobs in the animal world, and duties are much less physically taxing than many other careers with animals. Regular working hours and benefits are the norm. And it can be immensely gratifying to participate in research that may benefit the public and even save lives in the long run.

Although you will probably make a better salary in research than in other animal fields, your hands-on experience with animals will change. You are no longer helping animals directly, and you may need to perform experiments after which animals are ultimately euthanized. Some find the work monotonous, particularly dealing with administrative duties and the strict rules and regulations involved in conducting research. Another issue to consider is allergies, which can develop after working with large numbers of the same types of animals in a lab setting.

An Inside Look: Research Study Manager

Odessa Giardino MS, CVT, RLATG, Research Study Manager, Wyeth Research

Odessa manages a staff of junior scientists who specialize in laboratory animal science. She oversees regulatory compliance regarding animal welfare and the humane care and use of animals in research facilities.

How did you get into this field?

I became interested after many years of veterinary clinical work as a certified veterinary technician. My college experience stimulated a desire to do research, so I began to work in pharmaceuticals. I found that my technical experience was very pertinent to research.

What are your hours?

Monday through Friday, 8:30 a.m. to 5 p.m.

What is a typical day for you?

I review animal protocols to ensure compliance. I conduct walk-throughs of the facility to both monitor the animal health of the colonies and oversee the animal enrichment programs. I also organize the education and training of animal care staff and research scientists by running wetlabs.

What do you like most about your job?
I enjoy the impact I have on ensuring the highest standard of health and welfare of the animals used in research. I know that I directly affect how they are treated, and I am able to educate the scientific staff on the federal mandates regarding the use of animals in research. I interact with the animals, and feel I can enrich their lives.

What do you like least about your job?
Dealing with people, some days.

Do you have plans to further your career?
I am happy where I am in my career right now. I plan to continue on this track and become more and more proactive in the area of regulatory compliance.

How has your career/field changed over time?
Seven years ago when I first started, there wasn't nearly the regulatory oversight that exits today. I know that I have a direct impact on the changes I see because I am very active in local and national committees that protect the welfare of animals used in research. There continues to be strong support through education in the laboratory animal science field and through the increase in board-certified lab animal veterinarians.

Do you have any advice for someone entering the same/similar career?
Only do it if you believe in the mission of the field and have true compassion for the animals. You need to be a proactive person and ready for some challenging environments.

Alternative Job Opportunities

CHAPTER 11

The possibilities to work with or for animals in almost any career are endless. If you're creative about drawing on your specific professional skills and interests, you may just end up with a rewarding animal career you may have never thought was possible. These alternative career tracks vary in educational requirements and experience needed.

Freelance Work

As veterinary clinics become larger and more specialized, many businesses have begun to rely on outside sources to develop their staff. A staff development coordinator should have a good working knowledge of veterinary work, as well as training in business and good public speaking skills. This person travels often, and is called on to provide a wide range of services, including training and development of staff or management, motivational ideas, or suggestions as to the use of space. Most people offering this type of service have experience in some similar consulting capacity; this career track offers the option of part-time work or it could become your main career.

Be creative: writing and speaking

Many jobs involving animals offer various writing opportunities. Professional journals solicit articles from those in the field, and many journals exclusively publish case studies or research to educate and promote discussion within the professional veterinary or scientific community. Biologists and scientists often write about their findings for journals and are often the source of current newspaper or magazine articles discussing their particular knowledge. There is a near-constant demand for books in all areas of animal interest.

Along the same vein, speaking gigs can be part of a career with animals. Speakers are often sought out to give talks at various scientific and veterinary conferences and are paid accordingly, depending on profession and the type of lecture given. Hands-on wet labs are popular at conferences and give professionals the chance to practice new skills in a learning environment.

Relief work

Many veterinary hospitals hire doctors and trained support staff to fill in positions on an as-needed basis. Days and number of hours worked may vary, and often includes emergency hours. Some jobs may be for one day or be a few steady weeks to fill in for a worker on an extended leave. You may be called in to substitute for a worker who has called out sick or to cover while the office holds its yearly holiday party. Compensation is usually slightly higher than what would normally be paid to the same worker at that job, because benefits are not usually included and it is assumed that the relief worker possess enough skills and knowledge to fill in without extensive training.

Pet Bereavement

Pet bereavement services are increasingly common; professionals such as psychotherapists or clinical social workers who have experienced the loss of their own pet are getting into specializing in the area of pet loss. Some communities offer training and certification to anyone involved with animals so that that person might offer bereavement services to their clients. Group meetings may be held in coordination with a local animal hospital or shelter and are usually offered free of charge to the individuals attending, and there are hotlines available for those who do not have access to a local group. Trained professionals offer comfort over the phone to callers.

Education

Teaching and training people as they work towards earning their certifications or degrees in all areas of the animal field is another viable career option for those who already have the relevant certification, licensing or degree. For example, if you are teaching a veterinary terminology course at a community college, you will need to be a credentialed technician. A biology teacher needs a college degree including courses in the biological sciences as well as a teaching certificate. University professors need at least a relevant master's degree, and many professors also carry out research as part of their agreement with the school. Research is typically funded by various sponsoring groups.

Sales

Salespeople in the medical and pet supply industries sell products including vaccines, medications, bandaging material, food, cleaners, leashes, and various supplies to businesses; companies represented include pharmaceutical, food, medical equipment, uniform, pet toys, grooming supplies and surgical instruments. These sales representatives develop relationships with animal hospitals, pet stores, groomers and kennels in order to promote the company's products.

To know the business and to develop contacts with purchasing agents, reps spend many of their days traveling. Salespeople may attend trade shows or conferences, where they display products and take orders. Though sales representatives do not necessarily possess medical knowledge or skills, they may need to learn about how certain medical equipment is used to demonstrate how it works to a client. Some companies that sell research, laboratory or other similar equipment, food or medications may hire a technician, veterinarian or other skilled professional to give the demonstrations and answer questions about the products.

On top of a basic salary, some reps earn commission.

Animal Advocate/Lobbyist

As society continues to redefine its view of animal ethics, advocate groups promoting animal rights and providing sanctuaries for abused animals have been developing at an increasing rate.

Who they are

The Animal Legal Defense Fund is a group that facilitates programs in the field of animal law in law schools and within the legal profession. It also works with law enforcement and prosecutors to seek maximum penalties for animal abusers. Towards this end, it has a litigation program that files lawsuits that stop the abuse of companion and industry animals.

Farm Sanctuary was founded in 1986 to combat the abuses of industrialized farming and to encourage awareness and understanding about the way farm animals are treated in factory farms. When Farm Sanctuary's investigative and advocacy campaigns uncover cruelty at factory farms, stockyards and slaughterhouses, their emergency rescue team helps bring the animals to safety. Animals are relocated to a 175-acre shelter in upstate New York or a 300-acre shelter in northern California, where lifelong care and rehabilitation is provided by staff and volunteers. Farm Sanctuary has grown to become the nation's leading farm animal protection organization, with thousands of supporters. Their rescue and public education efforts work in conjunction with their advocacy for laws and policies to prevent suffering of animals while promoting compassion within the food industry. By reaching out to legislators and businesses, they work to bring about landmark institutional reforms.

Founded in 1980, People for the Ethical Treatment of Animals (PETA) is one of the largest animal rights organizations in the world, enlisting more than a million members and supporters. PETA is dedicated to establishing and protecting the rights of all animals and operates under the simple principle that animals are not ours to eat, wear, experiment on, or use for entertainment. This group focuses on four areas in which the largest numbers of animals suffer the most intensely for the longest periods of time: factory farms, laboratories, the clothing trade, and the entertainment industry. Other causes it takes on include the cruel killing of beavers, birds and other "pests," and the abuse of backyard dogs.

What they do

These groups all work through public education, cruelty investigation, research, animal rescue, legislation, special events, celebrity involvement and protest campaigns as their animal protection work brings together members of the scientific, judicial and legislative communities to stop abusive practices. Aided by congressional involvement, consumer boycotts and international media coverage, long-term changes that improve the quality of life for and prevent the deaths of countless animals have been achieved. Jobs in these advocacy groups include lobbyists, lawyers, administrative office workers, graphic designers, event coordinators, web site designers and accountants. One route of entry into this field is the internship. Interns help promote the group's grassroots outreach programs, distribute educational material, conduct research and help with office work, such as creating written material for demonstrations or for the media, preparing mailings and answer phones. These organizations also call on volunteers to attend outreach activities, provide foster homes, transport animals needing medical care, conduct research or help with office work.

Pet Law

Animal law is a growing interest in the legal community. In most states, pets have been considered property in the eyes of the law, and finding a lawyer who would take on cases involving animals was difficult or even ridiculed. Most lawyers who did take on these cases passed up any monetary compensation, as there was little chance of recovering damages. Today, there are as many as 70 law schools offering courses in animal law. The American Bar Association created its first committee on animal law in 2004, and in the process created a serious view on the subject. Purdue University School of Veterinary Medicine offers a course in animal forensics to assist the law with cases involving animals.

Cases may involve dog bites, animal trusts, custody battles, veterinary malpractice and housing issues. Many lawyers now argue that pets are more than mere property, and there is an inherent value in the bond they develop with their owners. Abuse cases are winding up in favor of the animals, and penalties awarded increasingly involve emotional value rather than an animal's market value. People are also including pets in their wills and go as far as creating trusts through lawyers to ensure the care of their pets after they have died.

Media

TV and film

As technology continues to evolve, so does its ability to bring animal issues to the general public in an accessible and up-to-the-minute form. The Animal Planet and National Geographic channels have done more to promote different jobs within the animal world than any other media. Shows like *Emergency Vets*, *Animals Cops*, *The Dog Whisperer* and *The Crocodile Hunter* give people a glimpse of what it may be like to work in these jobs. But there are also opportunities for work on these programs, whether creating dialogue, narrating, filming, editing or producing.

Documentary films are another growing source of information and insight into the natural world. David Attenborough was one of the genre's pioneers, showing animals all over the world in their natural environments and using constantly evolving technology to do so.

Books and magazines

Naturalists who have written books about the animal world include Charles Darwin, Edward O. Wilson, and Jane Goodall, and books on behavior are numerous. James Thurber wrote about dogs he bonded with during different periods of his life, and James Herriott's depiction of the country veterinarian in his All Creatures series is still popular today. Even people who seemingly have no knowledge of the animal world write books on the topic. Matthew Scully, a former Bush speechwriter influenced by the lobbying he witnessed from the hunting and farming industry as they pushed for laws promoting their industries, penned a book, Dominion, questioning the animal ethics we possess as a society.

Magazines about animals are also growing in number. Specific magazines for one type of animal are increasingly common; witness *Cat Fancy*, *Dog Fancy*, and *Bird Talk* and *Reptiles* magazines. Writers who have knowledge of these subjects are sought for articles by magazines, newspapers and trade journals.

An Inside Look: *Nature* Producer

Bill Murphy, BA, MBA, series producer for the *Nature* Series, Thirteen/WNET New York

Bill develops and oversees the production of natural history programs for Thirteen/WNET's Nature series produced for PBS television.

How did you get into this field?

My first job after graduate school was in the business affairs department of Thirteen/WNET New York. I transferred to the production department after two years.

What are your hours?

I usually work a 9- to 10-hour day except when I'm on location.

What is a typical day for you?

I review program treatments, develop program content, raise co-production investment, negotiate production agreements, review rough cuts and final cuts of programs, oversee productions in the field and post-production in the studio.

What do you like most about your job?

The fascinating subjects, and always working on multiple programs at any given time. Also, I get to work with the best natural history filmmakers in the world.

What do you like least about your job?

Some of the administrative work that must be done with each program, like contracts.

How has your career and field changed over time?

Natural history filmmaking is always evolving. I must always be looking for a new way to tell a story that will captivate the audience's attention. I also have to keep up and make use of changing technology like high definition television, surround audio and new ways of distributing programs like video streaming, VOD and digital theatrical screenings.

Do you have any advice for someone entering the same/similar career?

This is a very competitive field, so seek out the best independent natural history filmmakers and convince them to hire you as an intern or production assistant just to get a foot in the door.

Conclusion

Working with animals is a dynamic experience where the days are never the same and lifelong learning is a given. Although some days can be physically and mentally exhausting, this career path provides the potentially unique opportunity to fill your life with acts of compassion toward animals. At the same time, for those who have contact with animals in their daily jobs, there is often an awakened sense of awe at the world around us, which gives meaning to our lives. Working with animals brings about a sense that you are doing something beneficial in the world and for the future. As we strive to make the lives of our animal companions in this world better and try to alleviate their suffering, we leave a message for future generations to carry on our work.

The world is becoming more industrialized and wild places are being lost at an alarming rate. But people can continue to try to hold on to their connection to nature by bringing animals into their lives and communities. And because of this, careers in these fields will continue to grow and change in many different ways. By keeping an open mind to opportunities available, you may find the job with animals that you've always dreamed of.

CAREERS

APPENDIX

VETERINARY AND ANIMAL CAREERS

Appendix

Professional Organizations

America Animal Hospital Association (AAHA)
12575 Bayaud Ave.
Lakewood CO 80228-0899
Phone: (800) 883-6301
Member Service Center (303) 986-2800
http://www.aahanet.org/

American Association for Laboratory Animal Science
9190 Crestwyn Hills Drive
Memphis TN 38125
Phone: (901) 754-8620
www.aalas.org

American Society of Animal Science
1111 N. Dunlap Ave
Savoy, IL 61874
Phone: (217) 356-9050
www.asas.org

American Veterinary Medical Association
1931 North Meacham Road, Suite 100
Schaumburg, IL 60173
Phone: (847) 925-8070
www.avma.org

Association for Pet Loss and Bereavement, Inc
http://www.aplb.org/

International Association of Canine Professionals (IACP)
P.O. Box 560156
Montverde, FL 34756-0156
Phone: (877) 843-4227
http://www.dogpro.org/

National Animal Control Association
P.O. Box 1480851
Kansas City, MO 64148-0851
http://www.nacanet.org

National Association of Veterinary Technicians in America (NAVTA)
PO Box 224
Battle Ground, IN 47920
Phone: (765) 742-2216
www.navta.net
(offers information on Veterinary Technician Specialties and contact information for each organization)

National Association of Professional Pet Sitters
15000 Commerce Parkway, Suite C
Mt. Laurel, New Jersey 08054
Phone: (856) 439-0324
http://www.petsitters.org

National Dog Groomers Association of America, Inc.
http://www.nationaldoggroomers.com/

Pet Care Services Association
1702 East Pikes Peak Ave.
Colorado Springs, CO 80909
Phone: (877) 570-7788
http://www.petcareservices.org

Professional United Pet Sitters
http://www.petsits.com/

United States Equestrian Federation, Inc
http://www.usef.org/

The Wildlife Society
http://www.wildlife.org/publications/index.cfm?tname=journal

Zoos & Aquariums Associations of America
8403 Colesville Rd.
Suite 710
Silver Spring, MD 20910-3314
Phone: (301) 562-0777
www.aza.org

Schools

Full online directory of veterinary and technical schools

http://www.a2zcolleges.com/veterinary_schools/index.html

Long-distance veterinary technician programs

Blue Ridge Community College

Box 80

One College Lane

Weyers Cave, VA 24486

Phone: (540) 234-9261

www.brcc.edu/vettech/

Cedar Valley College

3030 N. Dallas Avenue

Lancaster, TX 75134

Phone: (877) 353-3482

http://www.cedarvalleycollege.edu/

Northern Virginia Community College

4001 Wakefield Chapel Road

Annandale, VA 22003-3796

Phone: (703) 323-3000

www.nvcc.edu

Penn Foster Career School

Phone: (800) 275-4410

http://www.pennfoster.edu/

Purdue University

625 Harrison Street

West Lafayette, IN 47907

Phone: (765) 496-6579

www.vet.purdue.edu/vtdl/

St. Petersburg College
PO Box 13489
St. Petersburg, FL 33733
Phone: (727) 341-3653
www.spcollege.edu/

Long-distance grooming course

Nash Academy
http://www.nashacademy.com/index.html

Helpful Web Sites

For information on careers in agriculture:
www.Agcareers.com

Alpaca Owner and Breeders Association
http://www.alpacainfo.com/

Animal Legal Defense Fund
http://www.aldf.org/

Farm Sanctuary
http://www.farmsanctuary.org/

Humane Society of the United States
2100 L. Street NW
Washington DC 20037
Phone: (202) 452-1100
www.hsus.org

Kingsnake website: online community for reptile and amphibian enthusiasts
http://www.kingsnake.com/

North American Reptile Breeders Conference and Trade Show
http://www.narbc.com/htm_2001/dfw_index.htm

PETA website
www.peta.org

Veterinary support staff on line education source

www.VetMedTeam.com

Technician employment website

www.Wheretechsconnect.com

ASPCA

http://www.aspca.org/

Starting a business

Association for Enterprise Opportunity

http://www.microenterpriseworks.org/

Farmer's Tax Guide

www.irs.gov/pub/irs-pdf/p225.pdf

Women's Venture Fund

www.womensventurefund.org/

Recommended Reading

Animal Network: online source for animal magazines and information

www.animalnetwork.com/animalnetwork/

Cat Fancy Magazine:

www.catchannel.com

Dog Fancy Magazine:

www.dogchannel.com

Groomer to Groomer magazine

www.groomertogroomer.com/

House Rabbit Society

www.rabbit.org/

Reptiles Magazine

www.reptilesmagazine.com/reptiles/home.aspx

Veterinary Technician Journal

www.VetTechJournal.com

About the Author

Liz Stewart has been working in the animal field for over 21 years. She obtained her B.S. in Pre-Veterinary Science from Rutgers University and became the first credentialed technician in New Jersey to become certified in Emergency and Critical Care by AVECCT (Academy of Veterinary and Critical Care Technicians.) Liz has written for Veterinary Technician magazine and has lectured at national Veterinary Critical Care Society (VECCS) conferences. She currently manages over 70 employees in the ECC & In-Patient Care Services at the Oradell Animal Hospital in New Jersey.

Go For The
GOLD!

• Access to 1,000+ extended insider employer
snapshots

VAULT
> the most trusted name in career information™